Longman
PHOTO DICTIONARY

Intermediate
Workbook

Marilyn S. Rosenthal
Daniel B. Freeman
Marjorie Fuchs

Longman Photo Dictionary Intermediate Workbook

Longman Inc., 95 Church Street, White Plains, N.Y. 10601

Associated companies:
Longman Group Ltd., London
Longman Cheshire Pty., Melbourne
Longman Paul Pty., Auckland
Copp Clark Pitman, Toronto
Pitman Publishing Inc., New York

Distributed in the United Kingdom by Longman Group Ltd., Longman House, Burnt Hill, Harlow, Essex CM20 2JE, England, and by associated companies, branches and representatives throughout the world.

Executive editor: Joanne Dresner
Development editor: Karen Davy
Production editor: Helen B. Ambrosio
Text & cover design: Joseph DePinho
Cover photo: John Edelman
Text art: Joseph DePinho, Martha Bradshaw, Beth Baum
Production supervisor: Helen B. Ambrosio

ISBN 0-8013-0056-8

89 90 91 92 93 9 8 7 6 5 4 3 2 1

CONTENTS

1 NUMBERS · TIME

1 **THE KENTUCKY DERBY.** The Kentucky Derby is the most famous horse race in the United States. Listen and write the positions of the horses as they run around the track.

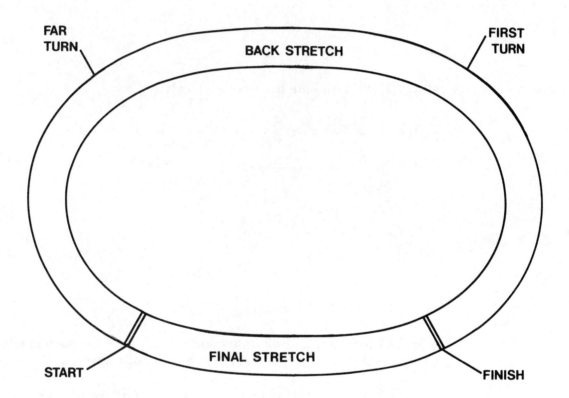

Horses' Names	Parts of the Track					
	Start	First Turn	Back Stretch	Far Turn	Final Stretch	Finish
Lucky Lady	1st					
Prince Charming	2nd	1st				
Fast Buck	3rd					
Mad Hatter	4th					

2 WHAT TIME IS IT? Write the times in words.

1. 6:45 _six forty-five_
2. 3:15 _____
3. 8:30 _____
4. 2:45 _____
5. 7:15 _____

6. 5:50 _____
7. 4:45 _____
8. 6:40 _____
9. 1:21 _____
10. 10:10 _____

3 FRACTIONS. Write the fractions in words.

1. 1/2 = _One half_
2. 1/4 = _____

3. 1/3 = _____
4. 3/4 = _____

4 A SECRET MESSAGE. Look at the code. Then write the correct letter for each number in the code to find out what the message says.

Code: 1 2 3 4 5 6 7 8 9 10 11 12 13 14 15 16 17 18 19 20 21 22 23 24 25 26
      A B C D E F G H I J K L M N O P Q R S T U V W X Y Z

23–5–12–3–15–13–5   20–15   20–8–9–19

W e l c o m e   ___ ___   _____

23–15–18–11–2–15–15–11   23–5   8–15–16–5   25–15–21

_____.   ___   _____   _____

12–9–11–5   9–20

_____   ___.

2

5 NUMBERS. Write the sentences in numbers.

1. One hundred divided by two is fifty. _$100 \div 2 = 50$_

2. Fifty-five percent plus forty-five percent is one hundred percent.

   _____

3. Three quarters minus one quarter is one half. _____

4. Four times five is twenty. _____

5. Fifty divided by two is twenty-five. _____

6. Seventy-five percent plus twenty-five percent is 100 percent.

   _____

7. One quarter plus one half is three quarters. _____

8. One half minus one quarter is one quarter. _____

9. Fifty minus fifteen is thirty-five. _____

10. Three times thirty is ninety. _____

6 AN OPINION POLL. We asked 1,000 people this question: "Do you prefer a

digital watch ( ) or an analog watch ( )?"

Sixty percent said they liked an analog watch. Forty percent said they liked a digital watch. Fifty percent of the people were men, fifty percent were women.

Fifty-five percent of all the men liked a digital watch. Forty-five percent liked an analog watch.

Twenty-five percent of all the women liked a digital watch and seventy-five percent liked an analog watch.

Complete the chart. Write the numbers (#) next to the percents (%). For example, 50% of 1,000 people is 500 people.

Question	Total Number of People = 1,000	Percent of Men = 50% Number of Men = ____	Percent of Women = 50% Number of Women = ____
Do you prefer a digital watch?	40% # _____	55% # _____	25% # _____
Do you prefer an analog watch?	60% # _____	45% # _____	75% # _____

2 CALENDAR & HOLIDAYS

1   MAKING AN APPOINTMENT. Mrs. Rivera is making an appointment with Dr. Becker's office. Listen and fill in the blanks.

1. Dr. Becker can see Mrs. Rivera at two o'clock on

   _Tuesday_____ , January _____ .

2. Mrs. Rivera can't make the appointment on _____ .

3. Dr. Becker isn't in the office on _____ .

4. Dr. Becker is busy on _____ , January _____ .

5. The first appointment in the morning is _____ , February

   _____ at _____ A.M.

2   PUNCTUATION. Days of the week, months and holidays begin with a capital letter and are separated from each other in a sentence by a comma. Correct the sentences by using a capital letter or a comma.

1. My birthday is ᴀaugust 15ˏ1964.

2. Happy new year.

3. Merry christmas.

4. We celebrate independence day on july 4th.

5. School starts in september.

6. My favorite day is saturday.

7. We have a date for thursday the 28th of november.

8. Graduation is on sunday june 10 1990.

9. Happy mother's day.

10. Is thanksgiving on thursday november 24th?

3 AN APPLICATION FORM. Fill out the top part of the application form. Use numbers for dates (January 15, 1989 = 1/15/89).

Date of Application ___/___/___
(month/day/year)

Name: _____ Date of Birth ___/___/___
first   last

Address: _____

Mother's Name: _____ Date of Birth ___/___/___
first   last

Father's Name: _____ Date of Birth
first   last   ___/___/___

Job History:

Current Position: Title _____

4 WHAT'S YOUR FAVORITE HOLIDAY? Write about your favorite holiday and how you celebrate it in your country. You can use the ideas in the box.

watch a parade	give presents	sing songs
have a family dinner	go to church	go to a party
watch fireworks	don't go to school	don't go to work

My favorite holiday is _____ . It is a special day in

my country because we celebrate_____ . On

_____ , I usually _____ and

_____ . Sometimes I _____ . My

friends usually _____ . My family usually

_____ . I enjoy _____ very much

because _____ .

5 A PLANNING CALENDAR. Choose a month and write the dates in the circles. Then write all the holidays that come in the month you chose. Finally, fill in the spaces with at least seven things you want to do during the month.

YEAR _____

_____

MONTH _____

SUNDAY	MONDAY	TUESDAY	WEDNESDAY	THURSDAY	FRIDAY	SATURDAY
○	○	○	○	○	○	○
○	○	○	○	○	○	○
○	○	○	○	○	○	○
○	○	○	○	○	○	○
○	○	○	○	○	○	○

3 | WEATHER & SEASONS

1 RADIO WQRV.
Listen to the weather report and fill in the blanks.

The temperature at 7:00 A.M. is _____*32*_____ degrees Fahrenheit
                                        1

and _____ degrees Celsius. The sky is _____ and
          2   3

it's _____ . Afternoon temperatures will be around
        4

_____ degrees Fahrenheit, _____ degrees Celsius. Tonight
     5   6

will be _____ and _____ with temperatures
            7   8

dropping _____ _____ .
              9   10

Tomorrow will be _____ and _____ . Snow will
                        11   12

develop in the late morning. Be careful driving. It may be _____ ,
                                                                13

and some roads will be _____ .
                            14

On Sunday it will become _____ with temperatures rising
                                15

into the high _____ s .
                  16

The forecast for the next week shows _____ weather with
                                            17

highs in the _____ s . It looks like _____ is coming to
                  18   19

an end and _____ will soon be here.
                20

7

2 IS IT POSSIBLE? Read the sentences and write *P* next to the sentences that are possible and *I* next to the sentences that are impossible. Correct the sentences that are impossible.

1. _I_ It's hot and icy.

   It's cold and icy _____

2. _P_ It's 30 degrees and snowy.

   _____

3. _____ It's minus four degrees and rainy.

   _____

4. _____ It's 80 degrees, sunny and foggy.

   _____

5. _____ It's 60 degrees and icy.

   _____

6. _____ It's 50 degrees and rainy.

   _____

7. _____ It's 80 degrees and snowy.

   _____

8. _____ It's clear and stormy.

   _____

9. _____ It's windy and cold.

   _____

10. _____ It's 40 degrees and clear.

    _____

3 MY FAVORITE SEASON. Complete the paragraph. Use the words and numbers in the box.

A	B	C	D		E	F
spring	sunny	warm	10	60	Fahrenheit	walk in the rain
summer	snowy	hot	20	70		go to the beach
winter	rainy	cold	30	80	Celsius	walk in the snow
fall	clear	cool	40	90		look at the leaves
	windy		50	100		smell the flowers

My favorite season is _____ . In the _____ , the weather is
                  (A)   (A)

usually _____ and _____ . I love _____ days when
        (B)   (C)   (B or C)

the temperature is about _____ degrees _____ . On
                   (D)   (E)

those days, I like to _____ .
                   (F)

4 HIDDEN WORDS. There are fourteen weather words in the box. Circle them.

C	L	O	U	D	Y	L	B	S	N	O	W	Y	A	J
L	C	E	R	Y	P	O	O	U	C	Q	I	S	C	V
E	X	C	V	B	A	S	D	N	H	G	N	P	O	I
A	D	V	D	C	R	E	R	N	I	E	D	X	P	O
R	O	L	B	F	O	G	G	Y	L	E	Y	M	O	L
E	R	S	F	W	I	A	C	B	L	T	Y	U	I	O
W	R	T	Y	A	R	A	I	N	Y	Z	C	B	I	L
Q	W	E	D	R	H	U	I	O	P	H	O	T	C	G
S	T	O	R	M	Y	G	H	O	U	E	L	W	Y	P
P	O	M	K	L	G	F	D	E	R	T	D	V	C	V
A	X	F	R	E	E	Z	I	N	G	O	B	K	O	I

4 SHAPES & MEASUREMENTS

 1   **A MYSTERY DRAWING. Listen and follow the directions.***

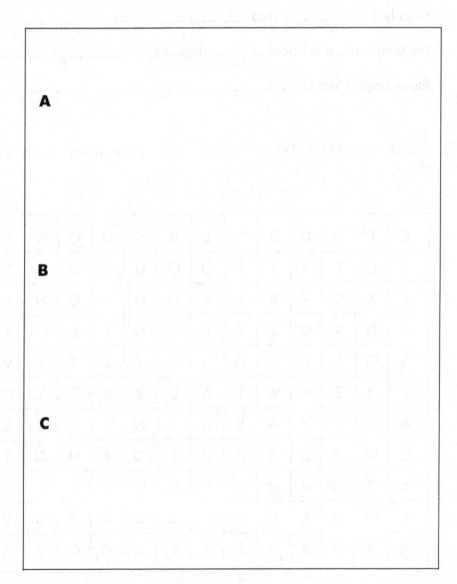

A

B

C

*A helpful hint: This line is one inch long: _____

2 HOW LARGE IS IT? Look at the abbreviations in the box. Then read the ads and fill in the blanks. Do not use abbreviations.

height = ht.	high = h.	feet = ft. or '
width = wdth.	wide = w.	inches = in. or "
depth = dpth.	deep = d.	
length = lgth.	long = l.	

1. **FOR SALE Couch:** lgth. 7' 9", wdth. 4'

The _length_ of the couch is 7 _feet_ 9 _inches_ . The _width_ of the couch is 4 _feet_ .

2. **Bookcase for Sale** 6' h., 2' d., 4' 2" w.

The bookcase is 6 _feet_ _high_ , 2 _feet_ _deep_ and 4 _feet_ 2 _inches_ _wide_ .

3. **Coffee Table for Sale** 17" h., 4' 3" l., 2' 1" w.

The coffee table is 17 _____ _____ 4 _____ 3 _____ _____ and 2 _____ 1 _____ _____ .

4. **Dining Room Table:** ht. = 27 in., wdth. = 3 ft. 2 in., dpth. = 3 ft.

The dining room table is 27 _____ _____ . The _____ of the table is 3 _____ 2 _____ . The _____ is 3 _____ .

5. **Oil painting for Sale** 2' 2" w., 3' 4" l.

The oil painting is 2 _____ 2 _____ and 3 _____ 4 _____ _____ .

6. **FOR SALE—Fish Tank:** ht. 15", wdth. 25", dpth. 12"

The _____ of the fish tank is 15 _____ . The _____ is 25 _____ and the _____ is 12 _____ .

11

3 GEOMETRY. Follow the directions.

1. Draw a triangle inside the circle.

2. Draw a line perpendicular to line A.   A

3. Draw a line parallel to line A.   A

4. Draw the radius of the circle.

5. Draw the diameter of the circle.

6. Draw the diagonal of the rectangle.

7. Put an X on the right angle of the triangle.

8. Put an X on the apex of the isosceles triangle.

9. Draw a spiral in the square.

10. Put an X on the front of the cube.

5 MONEY & BANKING

1 THE JEFFERSON BANK. Listen to the radio ad for the Jefferson Bank. Then read the sentences and write *True* or *False*.

1. The Jefferson Bank offers only Visa® and MasterCard®. *false*

2. You can get a green checkbook. _____

3. You can get traveler's checks and money orders from the computer.

   _____

4. The monthly statement shows all your deposits and withdrawals.

   _____

5. You can keep your important papers in the bank's vault. _____

6. You can use the cash machine 24 hours a day. _____

7. You can use the cash machine six days a week. _____

8. You need $100.00 to open an account at the Jefferson Bank. _____

2 MAKING CHANGE. Match the amounts in column A with the amounts in column B.

A		**B**
1. dollar	*a*	a. four quarters
2. quarter	_____	b. four twenties and two tens
3. five dollars	_____	c. two fives
4. ten dollars	_____	d. five ones
5. twenty dollars	_____	e. two dimes and a nickel
6. one hundred dollars	_____	f. two tens

3 **HOW WOULD YOU PAY? Look at the pictures. Then write the letters of the coins or bills you would use to pay for each item. Use as few coins or bills as possible.**

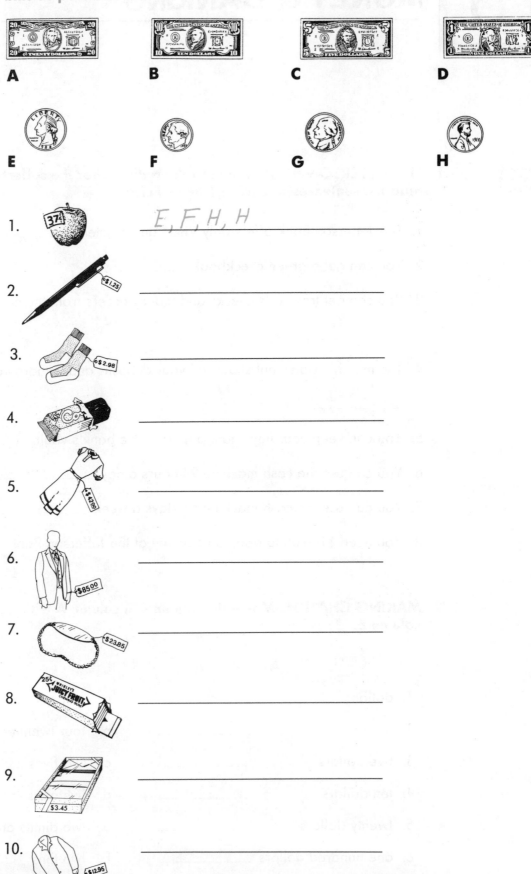

1. _E, F, H, H_____

2. _____

3. _____

4. _____

5. _____

6. _____

7. _____

8. _____

9. _____

10. _____

4 PAYING THE BILLS. You have eight bills to pay, but you have only $650.00 in your checking account. Choose the bills you can pay. Then write the checks.

BILLS TO PAY

Dr. Fred Cummings—office visit	$ 75
Allegheny Electric Co.—electricity, gas	$ 55
Sloan Management Co.—rent	$450
P and A Grocery Store—food	$ 85.25
California Telephone Co.—phone	$ 42.80
Alpha Furniture Co.—table	$137.50
Dresser Dry Cleaning—cleaning, laundry	$ 18.75
Visa Card—credit payment	$ 32.65

_____19___

Pay to the
Order of _Dr. Fred Cummings_ $ 75.00

Seventy five and no/100 _____ Dollars

JEFFERSON BANK

For _Office visit_ _____

_____19___

Pay to the
Order of _____ $ _____

_____ Dollars

JEFFERSON BANK

For _____ _____

_____19___

Pay to the
Order of _____ $ _____

_____ Dollars

JEFFERSON BANK

For _____ _____

_____19___

Pay to the
Order of _____ $ _____

_____ Dollars

JEFFERSON BANK

For _____ _____

_____19___

Pay to the
Order of _____ $ _____

_____ Dollars

JEFFERSON BANK

For _____ _____

6 THE WORLD
THE UNITED STATES · CANADA

 1 WORLD WIDE TOURS. Listen to the radio ad for World Wide Tours. On the map, write the names of the countries and oceans you hear.

2 CONTINENTS. Write the names of the continents.

1. France   *Europe* _____

2. Russia/USSR _____

3. Bulgaria _____

4. Morocco _____

5. Japan _____

6. Paraguay _____

7. Canada _____

8. China _____

9. Brazil _____

10. Greece _____

11. United States _____

12. Taiwan _____

13. Kenya _____

14. Saudi Arabia _____

3 LOCATION. Complete the sentences with the words *north*, *east*, *south* or *west*.

The United States

1. California is _south_ of Oregon and _west_ of Nevada.

2. Alabama is _____ of Mississippi, _____ of Georgia and _____ of Tennessee.

3. Texas is _____ of New Mexico, _____ of Oklahoma and _____ of Louisiana.

4. New York is _____ of Massachusetts and _____ of Pennsylvania.

5. Indiana is _____ of Ohio, _____ of Kentucky, _____ of Illinois and _____ of Michigan.

Canada

6. Ontario is _____ of Manitoba and _____ of Quebec.

7. Alberta is _____ of Saskatchewan, _____ of British Columbia and _____ of the Northwest Territories.

8. Victoria Island is _____ of Queen Elizabeth Islands and _____ of Baffin Island.

4 THE UNITED STATES. Look at the map and write the names of the states next to the abbreviations.

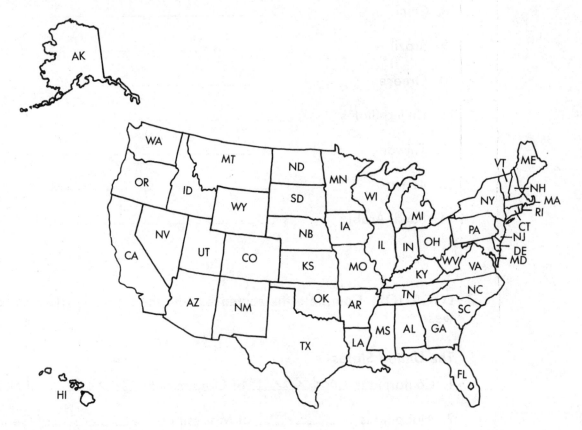

1. CA = *California*

2. NV = _____

3. WY = _____

4. AZ = _____

5. NM = _____

6. ND = _____

7. NB = _____

8. TX = _____

9. MO = _____

10. LA = _____

11. IL = _____

12. MI = _____

13. IN = _____

14. TN = _____

15. MS = _____

16. FL = _____

17. WV = _____

18. SC = _____

19. MD = _____

20. NJ = _____

21. NY = _____

22. CT = _____

23. MA = _____

24. ME = _____

25. HI = _____

7 THE CITY

1 **RADIO WQRV. Listen to the traffic report and put a check next to the picture that shows what people in Meadville should do today.**

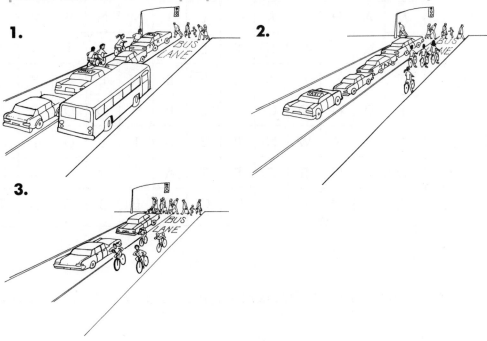

1.

2.

3.

2 **COMBINING WORDS. Combine words in the list to make new words or expressions. You can use the words more than once.**

can	office	booth	light
bus	walk	building	stand
sign	traffic	side	trash
phone	stop	lane	news

1. *trash can*

2. _____

3. _____

4. _____

5. _____

6. _____

7. _____

8. _____

9. _____

10. _____

3 HIDDEN WORDS. There are eleven city words in the box. Circle them.

S	S	T	F	D	E	B	U	S	L	M	R	G	O	C
U	A	U	M	O	O	T	H	T	A	X	K	O	N	U
B	H	T	B	V	Y	G	J	R	N	P	O	G	L	R
W	Y	R	C	T	S	L	K	E	E	X	I	T	J	B
A	D	A	V	A	A	P	Y	E	Q	I	A	G	L	T
Y	R	S	J	L	C	Y	O	T	R	A	F	F	I	C
M	A	H	S	K	G	L	I	M	N	B	V	L	X	Z
U	N	C	C	S	P	E	D	E	S	T	R	I	A	N
T	T	A	E	I	Z	R	B	W	E	S	P	O	I	G
F	D	N	Q	G	K	C	R	H	O	D	F	S	A	K
L	C	I	W	N	B	B	U	I	L	D	I	N	G	C
D	V	N	B	C	E	T	A	R	M	U	T	H	D	E
A	I	O	E	P	H	O	N	E	B	O	O	T	H	G

4 WHAT'S THE CATEGORY? Put the words into the correct category.

bus	taxi	sidewalk
office building	subway	street
traffic light	curb	car
skyscraper	crosswalk	street light

A. You can ride in it.   **B. You can walk on it.**   **C. You can look up at it.**

1. _bus_

1. _____

1. _____

2. _____

2. _____

2. _____

3. _____

3. _____

3. _____

4. _____

4. _____

4. _____

5 A QUESTIONNAIRE. Fill out the questionnaire about the city you live in or a city you know.

Questionnaire			

Name _____ Name of City _____ Name of Country _____

	Yes	No	Not Sure
1. Do you like this city?			
2. Is it a beautiful city?			
3. Do you have many friends in this city?			
4. Is it a big city?			
5. Are there many parking lots in this city?			
6. Are there any skyscrapers?			
7. Are there more than 50 office buildings?			
8. Are there traffic lights on every corner?			
9. Are there crosswalks for pedestrians?			
10. Are there parking meters?			
11. Are there subways?			
12. Are there buses?			
13. Do most people ride buses?			
14. Are there many newsstands?			
15. Are there many fire hydrants?			
16. Are there trash cans on every corner?			
17. Do you recommend this city to tourists?			

Tell why you like or don't like this city:

_____

_____

8 THE SUPERMARKET FRUIT · VEGETABLES

1 **A SHOPPING LIST. Juan and María are going to the supermarket. Listen and put a check next to the items they're going to buy.**

☑ roast	☐ frozen orange juice	☐ celery
☐ pork chops	☐ frozen vegetables	☐ potatoes
☐ chicken	☐ frozen dinners	☐ cabbage
☐ bacon	☐ tuna fish	☐ turnips
☐ steak	☐ soup	☐ carrots
☐ milk	☐ bread	☐ grapes
☐ eggs	☐ crackers	☐ bananas
☐ butter	☐ cookies	☐ strawberries
☐ cheese	☐ cereal	☐ mangoes
☐ yogurt	☐ lettuce	☐ peaches

2 **FRUIT AND VEGETABLES. Complete the sentences.**

1. _____ are my favorite fruit.

2. _____ are my least favorite fruit.

3. I have never eaten _____ .

4. I would like to try _____ .

5. I would not like to try _____ .

6. _____ is / are my favorite vegetable.

7. _____ is / are my least favorite vegetable.

8. I have never eaten _____ .

9. I would like to try _____ .

10. I would not like to try _____ .

3 YOUR SHOPPING LIST. Pretend you are going to the supermarket. You need to buy enough food for a week. Write your shopping list. You can buy anything you want.

Dairy

Frozen Foods

Canned Foods

Meat and Poultry

Packaged Goods

Fruit

Vegetables

THE MENU
FAST FOODS & SNACKS

1 **AT A RESTAURANT.** Lisa and Peter are at a restaurant. Listen and write what they order for dinner.

LISA	**PETER**

LISA	PETER
Appetizer _fruit cup_	Appetizer _____
Soup or Salad _____	Soup or Salad _____
Main Course _____	Main Course _____
Dessert _____	Dessert _____
Beverage _____	Beverage _____

2 **WHAT WOULD YOU LIKE FOR DINNER?** Look at the photos on page 17 of your PHOTO DICTIONARY and write what you would order from the menu. Choose one item from each group.

1. Appetizer _____

2. Soup or Salad _____

3. Main Course _____

4. Dessert _____

5. Beverage _____

3 ODD MAN OUT. Cross out the word that does not belong.

1. tomato juice   shrimp cocktail   ~~jello~~   fruit cup
2. popcorn   onion   tortilla chips   pretzels
3. donut   mustard   ketchup   relish
4. roast beef sandwich   gum   pizza   fried chicken
5. coffee   milk shake   soda   soup
6. apple pie   carrots   chocolate cake   ice cream
7. baked potato   stuffed tomatoes   green beans   fish
8. fish   roast beef   pork chops   hamburger

4 SCRAMBLED WORDS. Unscramble the words. Then put a check (√) next to the items you like and don't like.

		Like	Don't Like
1. zipaz	_pizza_	___	___
2. ketas	_____	___	___
3. eip	_____	___	___
4. aet	_____	___	___
5. sipleck	_____	___	___
6. shif	_____	___	___
7. tagipesht	_____	___	___
8. reneg banes	_____	___	___
9. sinono	_____	___	___
10. mahgerurb	_____	___	___
11. tho ogd	_____	___	___
12. dalas	_____	___	___

5 CALORIE COUNT. Look at the chart and complete the sentences.

1. According to the chart, the beverage with the fewest calories is

   _____tea_____ .

2. The beverage with the most calories is _____ .

3. If you compare one lb of fish, steak and chicken, you can see that

   _____ has the most calories. Fish has about sixty fewer

   calories than _____ .

4. According to the chart, the vegetable with the most calories is

   _____ .

5. A piece of apple pie with ice cream has _____

   calories.

6. A _____ is the dessert with the fewest calories.

Food	Amount	Calories
	1 cup	5
	1 cup	4
	1 cup	94
	1 lb	358
	1 lb	1316
	1 lb	394
	1	423
	1 cup	40
	1 cup	48
	1 cup	31
	1 cup	269
	1 piece	410
	1	125

10 THE POST OFFICE
THE OFFICE

1 AT THE OFFICE. Agnes is asking her secretary, Mary, to do some things for her. Listen and answer the questions.

1. Is Mary mailing the package to a man or a woman? _a man_

2. Is Mary sending the package express mail or certified mail?

   _____

3. Is Mary mailing the letter express mail or certified mail?

   _____

4. How many rolls of stamps is Mary getting? _____

5. How many books of stamps is Mary getting? _____

6. How many file folders is Mary getting at the stationery store?

   _____

7. How many message pads is she getting? _____

8. What else is Mary getting at the stationery store? _____

2 WHAT IS IT? Look at the pictures and complete the sentences.

1. You can put pencils in a _pencil holder_ .

2. You can put paper clips in a _____ .

3. You can put typing paper in a _____ .

4. You can put staples in a _____ .

5. You can put files in a _____ .

6. You can put tape in a _____ .

3 ADDRESSING ENVELOPES. Look at the abbreviations in the box. Then choose two people from the list and address the envelopes. Use abbreviations. (Turn to page 18 of this workbook for a list of abbreviations of states.) Be sure to write your return address in the left-hand corner of the envelopes.

(Turn to page 18 of this workbook for a list of abbreviations of states.)

Street = St.	Boulevard = Blvd.
Avenue = Ave.	Drive = Dr.
Road = Rd.	Apartment = Apt.
Parkway = Pkwy.	

Mr. Andrew Diamond
240 Kendrick Road
Newton, Massachusetts 02483

Ms. Ann Wallace
336 West End Avenue, Apartment 3C
New York, New York 10023

Mr. Dale Harvey
828 Chauncey Street
Baltimore, Maryland 21217

Ms. Noriko Korino
6048 Thorndike Drive
Oakland, California 94611

Mr. Juan Gómez
523 Harding Boulevard, Apartment 10F
Providence, Rhode Island 02902

Dr. Ronald Li
14 Henry Hudson Parkway
Chicago, Illinois 51436

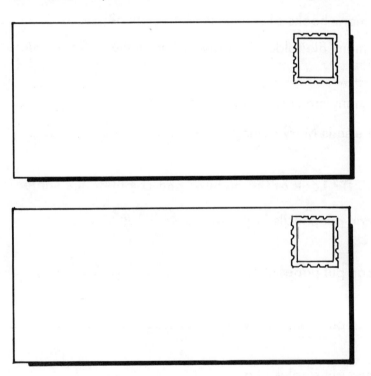

4 TRUE OR FALSE? Read the sentences. Then look at the first two photos on page 20 of your PHOTO DICTIONARY and write <u>True</u> or <u>False</u>. Correct the false sentences.

1. The typing paper is in the in box.

   False. It's in the typewriter.

2. The tape dispenser is between the stapler and the Rolodex.

   _____

3. The wastepaper basket is on the desk.

   _____

4. The file cabinet is in front of the secretary.

   _____

5. The Rolodex is next to the stationery.

   _____

6. The typewriter is on the file cabinet.

   _____

7. The note pad is to the left of the message pad.

   _____

8. The plant is on the secretary's desk.

   _____

11 THE BODY
ACTION AT THE GYM

1 **WAKE UP YOUR BODY.** Joan Fander of Radio WQRV is teaching an exercise class. Look at the pictures. Then listen and put a check next to the pictures that show the exercises.

A   B

Exercise 1 ✓

Exercise 2

Exercise 3

Exercise 4

Exercise 5

Exercise 6

Exercise 7

Exercise 8

2 WHAT GOES TOGETHER? Complete the analogies.

1. eye: *face* = nail:finger

2. finger:_____ = toe:foot

3. _____ :leg = hand:arm

4. elbow:arm = _____ :leg

5. eyebrow:eye = moustache:_____

6. ankle:leg = _____ :arm

7. forearm:_____ = calf:leg

3 MAKE YOUR OWN MONSTER. Complete the story about BRUCE, the monster. Choose any word you want to fill in the blanks. Write the correct form of the word. Do not use a word more than once. When you are finished, draw a picture of BRUCE.

Bruce is nine feet tall. He has three *heads* . His _____ are
head / arm / leg   tooth / eye

brown, and there is fire coming out of his _____ . He has red
                                            nose / ear / eye / mouth

hair all over his _____ . He has six _____ and only two
                  tooth / body / face   finger / toe

_____ .
finger / toe

31

4 TRUE OR FALSE? Read the sentences. Then look at the photos on page 27 of your PHOTO DICTIONARY and write <u>True</u> or <u>False</u>. Correct the sentences that are false.

Pictures 1–5

1. The man with glasses is bending.

False. He's stretching.

Pictures 6–8

2. The man on the left is bending.

_____

3. The man on the right is hopping.

_____

4. The woman is jumping.

_____

Pictures 9–10

5. The woman on the left is sitting.

_____

6. The woman on the right is reaching.

_____

Pictures 11–12

7. The woman is throwing the ball.

_____

8. The man is catching the ball.

_____

Pictures 13–15

9. The man on the left is pulling the table.

_____

10. The man in the middle is lifting something.

_____

12 COSMETICS & TOILETRIES ACTION AT HOME

 1 **A MAKEUP LESSON.** Cassandra Alexandra of Radio WQRV is giving some helpful hints for putting on makeup. Listen and write the numbers and the names of the cosmetics she talks about.

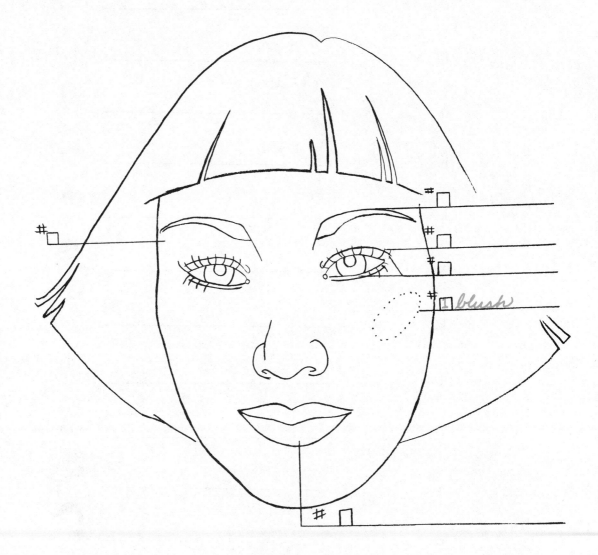

2 WHAT DO YOU DO EVERY DAY? Number the pictures to show the order in which you do these activities every day. Do not number activities you do not do. Then describe the pictures.

a. ___ I dry off.

b. ___ _____

c. ___ _____

d. ___ _____

e. _1_ I wake up

f. ___ _____

g. ___ _____

h. ___ _____

i. ___ _____

j. ___ _____

k. ___ _____

l. ___ _____

m. ___ _____

n. ___ _____

o. ___ _____

p. ___ _____

3 A TYPICAL MORNING. Complete the story about a typical morning in the life of a friend or relative. You can use the ideas in the box. Be sure to use the correct verb forms.

take a shower	brush his / her hair	shampoo his / her hair
brush his / her teeth	comb his / her hair	wash his / her face
shave	take a bath	eat breakfast
put on her makeup	put on cologne	

_____ 's Morning
(name of friend or relative)

_____ usually wakes up at
(name)

_____ . First _____ _____
(time)   (he / she)

_____ . Then _____ _____
                                              (he / she)

_____ . After _____ _____
                                               (he / she)

_____ , _____ usually _____
                                 (he / she)

_____ and _____ .

_____ then _____ and _____
(He / She)

_____ . When _____ finishes all this,
                                        (he / she)

_____ goes out.
(he / she)

4 ODD MAN OUT. Cross out the word that does not belong.

1. foundation   blush   ~~nail polish~~   lipstick

2. lipstick   eye shadow   eyeliner   mascara

3. shampoo   brush   comb   cologne

4. hair tonic   cologne   brush   after-shave

5. nail polish   after-shave   eyebrow pencil   mascara

6. comb   nail file   nail clipper   emery board

13 | ACTION AT SCHOOL

1 **IN THE CLASSROOM.** Mrs. Rodríguez is talking to her class. Listen and match the students' names in column A with the pictures in column B.

A	B
1. _c_ John	a.
2. ___ Jane	b.
3. ___ Mary	c.
4. ___ Steven	d.
5. ___ Lisa	e.
6. ___ Anne	f.
7. ___ Beth	g.
8. ___ Tim	h.
9. ___ Rick	i.
10. ___ Laura	j.

2 **WHAT DO STUDENTS DO?** Write sentences about students in your school. Use any of the verbs in the box.

write	smile	laugh	read
frown	paint	sculpt	draw

1. _____

2. _____

3. _____

3 **DESCRIBING. Look at the top photo on page 28 of your PHOTO DICTIONARY and complete the paragraph.**

The student in the blue shirt is _writing_ a math problem on the

blackboard. The teacher is _____₂ to one of the answers. The girl

next to the teacher is _____₃ the board. The girl in the blue

sweater is _____₄ a notebook to the boy next to her, and he is

_____₅ it. The boy in front of her is _____₆ a book.

The boy next to him is _____₇ a piece of

paper. The girl behind him is _____₈ a piece

of paper.

4 **TRUE OR FALSE? Look at the middle photo on page 28 of your PHOTO DICTIONARY. Then read the sentences and write <u>True</u> or <u>False</u>. Correct the sentences that are false.**

1. The girl on the left is drawing.

   False. She's painting.

2. The man on the left is sitting.

   _____

3. The girl in the middle is sculpting.

   _____

4. The boy in the red sweater is picking up a piece of paper.

   _____

5. The boy on the right is writing.

   _____

14 THE DOCTOR THE DENTIST

1 **WHERE ARE THEY? Where do the conversations take place? Listen and put a check in the correct column.**

	The Doctor's	The Dentist's
1.	✓	
2.		
3.		
4.		
5.		
6.		
7.		
8.		

2 **DEFINITIONS. Fill in the blanks with the words in the box.**

toothpaste	thermometer	x-ray
~~tissue~~	scale	

1. You use it to blow your nose. _tissue_

2. It measures your weight. _____

3. It takes a picture of your bones. _____

4. It measures your body temperature. _____

5. You put it on a toothbrush. _____

3 AT THE DENTIST'S OFFICE. Look at page 30 of your PHOTO DICTIONARY and fill in the blanks.

Most people hate to go to the <u>d</u> <u>e</u> <u>n</u> <u>t</u> <u>i</u> <u>s</u> <u>t</u> .
                                                              1

Sheila doesn't agree. She likes to go to her dentist's office.

Dr. Chui is very kind, and his ___ ___ ___ ___ ___ <u>l</u>

___ ___ ___ ___ <u>s</u> <u>t</u> ___ ___ ___ , Clare, is too.
                              2

Dr. Chui always knows how to help his patients. If Sheila

needs a ___ ___ <u>l</u> ___ ___ ___ , Dr. Chui gives
                          3

her ___ ___ <u>v</u> ___ ___ ___ ___ before he
                    4

uses the ___ ___ <u>i</u> ___ ___ . When Sheila
                    5

had an ___ ___ ___ <u>b</u> ___ ___ ___ ,
                      6

Dr. Chui made ___ <u>r</u> ___ ___ ___ ___ for her and
                    7

now her teeth are straight.

4 SENTENCE + SENTENCE = SENTENCE. Combine the pairs of sentences to make new sentences.

1. { I had a headache.
   { I took an aspirin.

   I took an aspirin for my headache.

2. { I had high blood pressure.
   { The doctor gave me a prescription.

   _____

3. { She had food between her teeth.
   { She used dental floss.

   _____

4. { He had a cut.
   { He used a Band-Aid.

   _____

15 | OCCUPATIONS THE FAMILY · EMOTIONS

1 **WHAT ARE YOU GOING TO DO?** María, Lisa and Kenji are high school students. They're talking about what they're going to do after graduation. Listen and fill in the blanks.

1. Lisa is going to be a _Secretary_ in her _____ office.

2. Her _____ is happy, but her _____ is _____ because she wants Lisa to be a _____ .

3. Kenji is going to be a _____ _____ .

4. His _____ is very _____ of him.

5. Kenji's _____ is an _____ .

6. _____ doesn't know what she's going to do after she graduates. She's _____ .

7. María's father wants her to be a _____ , but her mother thinks she should be a _____ .

8. María's brothers want her to be a _____ , but she thinks she's too _____ .

9. Kenji's _____ Rita is a _____ , and she _____ her job.

10. María sometimes feels _____ when she's with people, so maybe she should be a _____ .

2 WHAT GOES TOGETHER? Complete the analogies.

1. father:son = _mother_ : daughter

2. grandfather:_____ = grandmother:mother

3. nephew:uncle = niece:_____

4. husband:brother-in-law = wife:_____

5. husband:_____ = wife:mother-in-law

6. grandfather:_____ = grandmother:

   granddaughter

7. father-in-law:son-in-law = mother in law:_____

3 OPPOSITES. Match the words in column A with their opposites in column B.

	A		B
1.	_C_ sad	a.	pleased
2.	___ proud	b.	miserable
3.	___ displeased	c.	happy
4.	___ ecstatic	d.	ashamed

Now write the words in the correct column.

Positive (+)	Negative (−)
proud	_____
_____	_____
_____	_____
_____	_____

4 YOUR FAMILY. Describe your relatives. Write the person's name, occupation and one emotion that describes the person (for example: happy, shy, etc.). Note: For people who work at home, write *homemaker* as the occupation. For students, write *student*.

Relative	Name	Occupation	Emotion
Grandfather			
Grandfather			
Grandmother			
Grandmother			
Father			
Mother			
Aunt			
Uncle			
Cousin			
Sister			
Brother			
Sister-in-law			
Brother-in-law			
Nephew			
Niece			
Son			
Daughter			

16 OPPOSITES

1 **AT THE POLICE STATION.** Mr. Prudente is very worried because his wife didn't come home from work today. He's talking to a police officer. Listen and put a check next to the correct picture.

1.  **2.**  **3.**  **4.**

2 **WHAT'S THE OPPOSITE? Complete the sentences.**

1. At 3:00 P.M. it's light, but at 3:00 A.M. it's _dark_ .

2. My daughter is clean when she goes to school, but she's _____ when she comes home.

3. February is a cold month in most of North America, but in many countries in South America, it's _____ .

4. Tomiko is putting a new Band-Aid on her cut. She's throwing the _____ Band-Aid in the wastepaper basket.

5. Your brother's room is neat. Why is your room _____ ?

6. The package is heavy, but the letter is _____ .

7. Carmelo has curly hair, but he uses a hair dryer to make it _____ .

8. The newsstand on the corner is closed, but the newsstand near the bus stop is _____ all night.

3 TRUE OR FALSE? Read the sentences and write True or False. Correct the false sentences.

1. A nail file is rougher than an emery board.

   False. A nail file is smoother than an emery board.

2. Cotton is softer than wood.

   _____

3. Horses are slower than dogs.

   _____

4. A rock is heavier than a feather.

   _____

5. A skyscraper is taller than a house.

   _____

6. A child is older than its mother.

   _____

7. Fire is colder than ice.

   _____

8. Day is lighter than night.

   _____

9. Cars are faster than planes.

   _____

10. Cats are younger than kittens.

    _____

11. February is longer than March.

    _____

12. Sidewalks are usually narrower than streets.

    _____

4 COMPARING. Look at the pictures and complete the sentences.

tall / short

1. Dan is _taller_ than Ann.

2. Ann is _____ than Dan.

3. Stan is the _tallest_ .

4. Ann is the _____ .

young / old

5. José is _____ than Sue.

6. Kim is _____ than José.

7. Kim is the _____ .

8. Sue is the _____ .

Now write five sentences comparing Oak Street, Elm Street and Main Street.

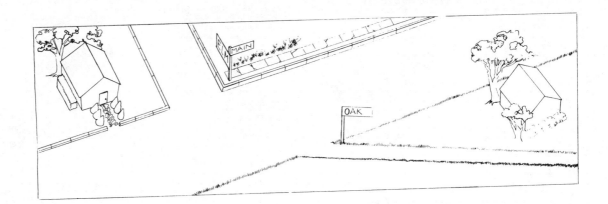

wide / narrow

9. _Oak Street is narrower than Elm Street._

10. _____

11. _____

12. _____

13. _____

17 MEN'S WEAR WOMEN'S WEAR

1 **A DESIGNER'S ADVICE. A fashion designer is talking on a TV show. Listen and put a check next to the pictures that show the clothes he thinks men should wear this year.**

Casual Wear

1.

2.

3.

Very Casual Wear

4.

5.

6.

Business Wear

7.

8.

9.

TRUE OR FALSE? Look at pages 35 and 36 of your PHOTO DICTIONARY. Then read the statements and write True or False. Correct the statements that are false.

Page 35

1. The man in photo A is wearing a red vest.

   False. He's wearing a red tie.

2. The man in photo B is wearing a tan sport coat.

   _____

3. The man on the right is wearing a striped sport shirt.

   _____

Page 36

4. In photo A, the woman on the right is carrying a handbag.

   _____

5. In photo A, the woman on the left is carrying a shoulder bag.

   _____

6. In photo B, the woman is wearing a skirt.

   _____

7. The girl in the blue t-shirt is wearing flowered shorts.

   _____

8. The knee socks are pink.

   _____

9. The tights are beige.

   _____

10. The girl in jeans is wearing a yellow blouse.

    _____

18 MEN'S & WOMEN'S WEAR ACCESSORIES

1 **THE SALE OF A LIFETIME!** Listen to the radio ad for Lacey's Department Store and put a check next to the items that are on sale. Then write the sale price.

Shoe Department

1. _____ 2. _____ 3. _$6.99_ 4. _____ 5. _____

Women's Department

6. _____ 7. _____ 8. _____

Jewelry Department

9. _____ 10. _____ 11. _____ 12. _____ 13. _____

Accessory Department

 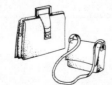

14. _____ 15. _____ 16. _____ 17. _____ 18. _____

48

2 **WHERE DO YOU WEAR IT? Complete the sentences. Use the words in the box.**

scarf	ring	sho̶e̶s
gloves	watch	cap

1. You wear _shoes_ on your feet.

2. You wear a _____ on your wrist.

3. You wear a _____ on your neck.

4. You wear a _____ on your finger.

5. You wear a _____ on your head.

6. You wear _____ on your hands.

3 **WORD + WORD = WORD. The words in the list are made up of two separate words. Look at the example: *hand + bag = handbag*. Circle the separate words in the list and use them to fill in the blanks in the sentences.**

earring	handbag
turtleneck	undershirt
raincoat	tiepin

1. My h a n d is cold.

2. He put his books in the b a g .

3. My __ a __ hurts.

4. Tom's __ __ e is blue

5. Joan wears a gold __ __ __ g on her finger and a gold chain around her

   __ __ __ k .

6. A t __ __ __ __ __ moves very slowly.

7. I love to walk in the __ __ __ n .

8. Mrs. Soto is wearing a beautiful __ i __ on her c __ __ __ __ .

9. You can't see the teacher's blue __ h __ __ __ because it's __ __ __ __ r

   his sweater.

19 HOUSING
THE BACKYARD AND GARDEN

1 **BUYING A HOUSE. Ginny and Bob Wilson want to buy a house. They're talking to a real-estate agent. Listen and put a check in the correct boxes.**

CITY LIGHTS REAL ESTATE
HOUSING QUESTIONNAIRE

Type of House or Building

☐ ranch   ☐ two-story
☐ two-family   ☐ apartment

Inside

☐ dining room   ☐ 3–4 bathrooms
☐ 1–2 bedrooms   ☐ large kitchen
☐ 3–4 bedrooms   ☐ large lobby
☐ 1–2 bathrooms   ☐ elevators

Outside

☐ garage   ☐ patio
☐ driveway   ☐ front yard
☐ porch   ☐ lawn
☐ balcony   ☐ backyard

Now put a check next to the house Ginny and Bob are going to see.

1.

2.

3.

2 HOUSING ADS. Look at the real-estate ads. Then read the statements and write True or False. Correct the statements that are false.

RANCH HOUSE FOR SALE All on one floor. 3 bedrooms, 2 bathrooms. large patio.	**APARTMENT FOR RENT** Elevator building, 5th floor. 1 bedroom, bathroom, kitchen, living room. Large balcony.
TWO-FAMILY HOUSE FOR SALE Upstairs and downstairs apartments. 2-car garage. Side door.	**TWO-STORY HOUSE FOR SALE** 5 bedrooms, 4 bathrooms. Dining room. Long driveway and 1-car garage. Large garden.

1. The ranch house has stairs.

   False. It's on one floor.

2. The ranch house has a garden.

   _____

3. The two-family house has a stairway.

   _____

4. The apartment has a balcony.

   _____

5. The two-story house has a patio.

   _____

6. The apartment is for sale.

   _____

7. The two-story house has a two-car garage.

   _____

8. The apartment is on the fifth floor.

   _____

3 DEFINITIONS. Fill in the blanks with the words in the box.

rake	trowel	barbecue
umbrella	elevator	watering can
lounge chair	closet	lawn mower

1. You collect leaves with it. _rake_

2. You mow the lawn with it. _____

3. You water flowers with it. _____

4. You plant flowers with it. _____

5. You cook meat on it. _____

6. You sit in the shade under it. _____

7. You sit on it. _____

8. You go upstairs in it. _____

9. You hang your clothes in it. _____

4 ODD MAN OUT. Cross out the word that does not belong.

1. rake   trowel   azalea   lawn mower

2. bush   watering can   hedge   flower bed

3. hedge   geranium   snapdragon   pansy

4. patio   balcony   porch   kitchen

5. living room   bathroom   garage   bedroom

6. roof   hall   chimney   shutters

20 THE LIVING ROOM THE DINING ROOM THE BEDROOM · THE BATHROOM

1 WHERE ARE THEY? Where do the conversations take place? Listen and put a check in the correct column.

	Living Room	Dining Room	Bedroom	Bathroom
1.	___	✓	___	___
2.	___	___	___	___
3.	___	___	___	___
4.	___	___	___	___
5.	___	___	___	___
6.	___	___	___	___
7.	___	___	___	___
8.	___	___	___	___

2 COMPARING. Write sentences making comparisons.

1. (big) living room/dining room

   A living room is bigger than a dining room.

2. (soft) mattress/the floor

   _____

3. (warm) sheet/quilt

   _____

4. (wide) hand towel/bath towel

   _____

3 A FURNITURE SALE. Look at the ad for living room furniture. Write in the missing information.

	Regular		Sale
Sofa	$ 1,300		$
Love seat	$		$
club chair	$450		$279
Ottoman	$		$
Coffee table	$		$
End table	$		$
	$900		$600
	$150		$75
Mirror	$		$
Carpet	$		$

4 **TRUE OR FALSE? Look at page 42 of your PHOTO DICTIONARY. Then read the sentences and write** <u>True</u> **or** <u>False</u>**. Correct the statements that are false.**

1. There are eight chairs around the dining room table.

False. There are six chairs around the dining room table.

2. The plant is next to the door.

_____

3. The centerpiece is made of flowers.

_____

4. The serving bowl is empty.

_____

5. The napkins are to the left of the plates.

_____

6. The drapes are paisley.

_____

7. There's a picture over the sideboard.

_____

8. There's a chandelier above the table.

_____

9. The knife is shorter than the soupspoon.

_____

21 THE KITCHEN KITCHENWARE

1 **IN THE KITCHEN.** Manny and Laura are going to make some coffee. Listen and put a check next to the items they use.

1.

2.

3.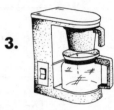

4.

5.

6.

7.

8.

9.

2 **COMPARING.** Write sentences making comparisons.

1. (cold) refrigerator/freezer

A freezer is colder than a refrigerator.

2. (fast) knife/food processor

_____

3. (heavy) plastic wrap/aluminum foil

_____

4. (slow) toaster oven/microwave oven

_____

3 IN THE KITCHEN. Complete the sentences.

1. You want to take something hot off the stove. You need a
   a. plate.
   b. freezer.
   c. pot holder. *(circled)*

2. You want some cold water. You turn on the
   a. counter.
   b. faucet.
   c. dishwasher.

3. You want to dry the dishes. You need a
   a. strainer.
   b. canister.
   c. towel.

4. Most stoves have four
   a. burners.
   b. drawers.
   c. trivets.

5. Another word for cupboard is
   a. range.
   b. skillet.
   c. cabinet.

6. You're hungry. You look in the
   a. sink.
   b. refrigerator.
   c. drawer.

7. You keep spices on a
   a. rack.
   b. saucer.
   c. trivet.

8. You can cook food quickly in a
   a. food processor.
   b. blender.
   c. microwave oven.

9. You CAN'T make toast in a
   a. toaster oven.
   b. toaster.
   c. roaster.

10. The pan is hot. You don't want to burn the counter. You need a
    a. trivet.
    b. cake stand.
    c. lid.

4 DEFINITIONS. Look at page 46 of your PHOTO DICTIONARY and fill in the blanks.

1. It's a tool with a wide flat blade for spreading, mixing or lifting soft substances.

   spatula

2. It's a large spoon with a long handle. _____

3. It's an instrument used for beating. _____

4. It's an instrument for separating solids from liquids. _____

5. It's a tool used for cutting. _____

6. It's a tool that removes the outer skin of a fruit or vegetable.

   _____

5 **DIFFERENCES. Look at the two kitchens. Can you find six differences between them?**

A   **B**

1. There's a dishwasher in kitchen A, but there isn't a dishwasher in kitchen B.

2. _____

_____

3. _____

_____

4. _____

_____

5. _____

_____

6. _____

_____

22 THE NURSERY THE PLAYGROUND

1 **WHAT'S ON SALE?** Listen to the radio ad for the Toddlers and Tots store.
Look at the pictures and cross out the incorrect information.

1.

$75.00

$55.00

2.

$150.00

$~~100~~.00

3.

$30.00

$25.00

red, blue, green, yellow

4.

$100.00

$ 75.00

red, blue, green, yellow

5.

$75.00

$55.00

6.

$150.00

$100.00

7.

$100.00

$ 75.00

2 WHAT IS IT? Fill in the blanks.

1. It's on a crib and rhymes with car.   B   A   (R)

2. It has drawers and rhymes with west.   ___ ___ ___ (O)

3. It's filled with sand and rhymes with nail.   ___ (O) ___ ___

4. It's high in the air and rhymes with light.   (O) ___ ___ ___

5. It's a kind of box and rhymes with hand.   ___ ___ (O) ___

6. They're on the baby and rhyme with nose.   ___ (O) ___ ___ ___

7. It gives you light and rhymes with stamp.   ___ (O) ___ ___

8. It's in the playground and rhymes with wide.   ___ ___ ___ (O)

9. It can be pushed and rhymes with ring.   (O) ___ ___ ___

10. It's sometimes a teddy and rhymes with hair.   (O) ___ ___

Now unscramble the letters in the circles.

___ ___ ___ ___ ___ ___ ___ ___ ___

23 THE LAUNDRY ROOM
TOOLS · CONSTRUCTION

1 WHAT'S HAPPENING? Listen and circle the correct answer.

1. What is the man going to do?
   a. Wash clothes.
   b. Dry clothes.
   c. Iron clothes.

2. What is the woman going to do?
   a. Put clothes in the dryer.
   b. Hang clothes in the closet.
   c. Hang clothes on the clothesline.

3. Where should the man look for his shirt?
   a. On a hanger.
   b. In the hamper.
   c. On the ironing board.

4. What else can the man use?
   a. A dust cloth.
   b. A carpet sweeper.
   c. A sponge mop.

5. What are they going to do with their clothes?
   a. Put them in the washing machine.
   b. Put them in the dryer.
   c. Hang them on the clothesline.

6. What is the man going to buy?
   a. Detergent.
   b. A bulb.
   c. An extension cord.

7. What does the woman need?
   a. A three-pronged plug.
   b. A bulb.
   c. An extension cord.

8. What does the man give the woman?
   a. A utility knife.
   b. A hammer.
   c. A tape measure.

9. What should the man use?
   a. A paint brush.
   b. Sandpaper.
   c. A roller.

10. What does the woman give the man?
    a. A tape measure.
    b. A folding rule.
    c. A wrench.

2 TRUE OR FALSE? Read the sentences. Then look at the first photo on page 49 of your PHOTO DICTIONARY and write True or False. Correct the sentences that are false.

1. The ironing board is red.

   False. It's blue).

2. The iron is on the ironing board.

   _____

3. The carpet sweeper is to the left of the vacuum cleaner.

   _____

4. The dust cloth is blue.

   _____

5. The sponge is in the bucket.

   _____

6. The carpet sweeper has a plug.

   _____

7. The dustpan is between the dust cloth and the whisk broom.

   _____

3 A BUILDING PUZZLE. Look at page 53 in your PHOTO DICTIONARY and fill in the blanks.

1. _____ S C A F F O L D _____

2. _____ H _____

3. _____ O _____

4. _____ V _____

5. _____ E _____

6. _____ L _____

ELECTRONICS

1 **THE BIGGEST SAVINGS IN TOWN.** Listen to the radio ad for Wild Willy's Electronics Shop. Look at the newspaper ad and put a check next to the items that are on sale.

WILD WILLY'S ELECTRONICS SHOP

TVs	$199.95
✓ VCRs	229.95
Turntables	89.95
Tuners	110.00
Amplifiers	180.00
Cassette Decks	189.00
Speakers	79.95
Compact Discs	12.99
Radios	24.95
Clock Radios	24.95
Cassette Players	59.00
Walkmans	21.95
Answering Machines	49.95
Telephones	34.95
Pocket Calculators	24.95
Electronic Typewriters	188.00
Electric Typewriters	98.00
Cameras	369.00
Video Cameras	1088.00
Slide Projectors	230.00

---

2 TRUE OR FALSE? Look at the newspaper ads. Then read the sentences and write True or False. Correct the sentences that are false.

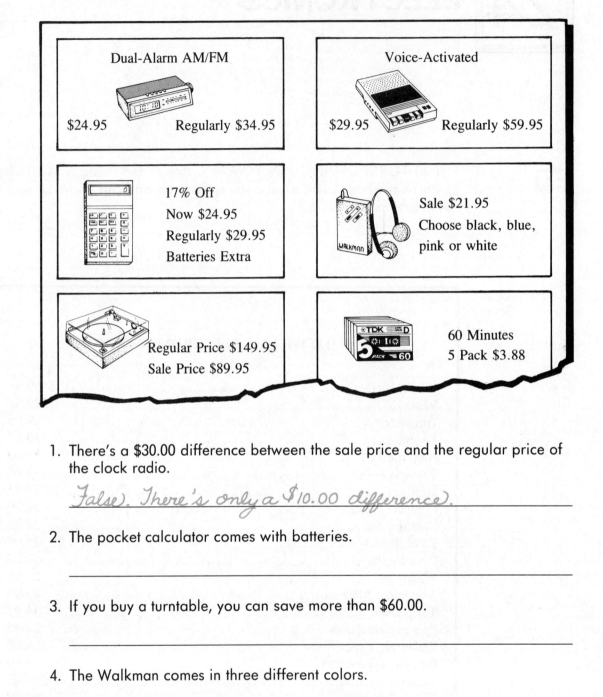

Dual-Alarm AM/FM

$24.95   Regularly $34.95

Voice-Activated

$29.95   Regularly $59.95

17% Off
Now $24.95
Regularly $29.95
Batteries Extra

Sale $21.95
Choose black, blue,
pink or white

Regular Price $149.95
Sale Price $89.95

60 Minutes
5 Pack $3.88

1. There's a $30.00 difference between the sale price and the regular price of the clock radio.

   False). There's only a $10.00 difference.

2. The pocket calculator comes with batteries.

   _____

3. If you buy a turntable, you can save more than $60.00.

   _____

4. The Walkman comes in three different colors.

   _____

5. The Walkman comes with headphones.

   _____

6. If you buy the cassette recorder and five cassettes, you'll pay $33.83.

   _____

3 A CROSSWORD PUZZLE. Complete the puzzle.

Across

1. You add numbers with it.
2. You use it to speak to people.
3. You take pictures with it.

Down

4. You put it in your camera.
5. You put a record on it.
6. You type on it.

4 ELECTRONIC EQUIPMENT. Make a list of electronic equipment that you have at home. Then make another list of the equipment you would like to have.

	Have	Would Like to Have
1.		
2.		
3.		
4.		
5.		
6.		
7.		
8.		

25 LAND & WATER

1 **WHERE ARE THEY?** Listen and circle the correct answer.

1. Where are the man and woman?
   a. In the desert.
   b. In the mountains.
   c. In a forest.

2. Where are the man and woman?
   a. On a cliff.
   b. In a forest.
   c. On a lake.

3. Where is the woman?
   a. In the desert.
   b. In a valley.
   c. On a cliff.

4. Where are the man and woman?
   a. In the desert.
   b. In a forest.
   c. In a meadow.

5. Where are the man and woman?
   a. On a cliff.
   b. In a meadow.
   c. In a brook.

6. Where are the man and woman?
   a. In a pond.
   b. In a lake.
   c. In a forest.

2 **WHAT IS IT?** Look at page 54 of your **PHOTO DICTIONARY** and fill in the blanks.

1. It's green and it rhymes with glass.   G R A S Ⓢ

2. It's hard and it rhymes with sock.   Ⓞ __ __ __

3. It's made of sand and it rhymes with spoon.   Ⓞ __ __ __

4. It's made of water and it rhymes with liver.   __ __ __ Ⓞ __

5. It's also water and it rhymes with cake.   __ __ __ Ⓞ

6. It moves and it rhymes with cream.   __ Ⓞ __ __ __

Now unscramble the letters in the circles. __ __ __ __ __

3 A GEOGRAPHY QUIZ. Look at the map and complete the sentences with the words in the box.

mountain	lake	waterfall
river	desert	

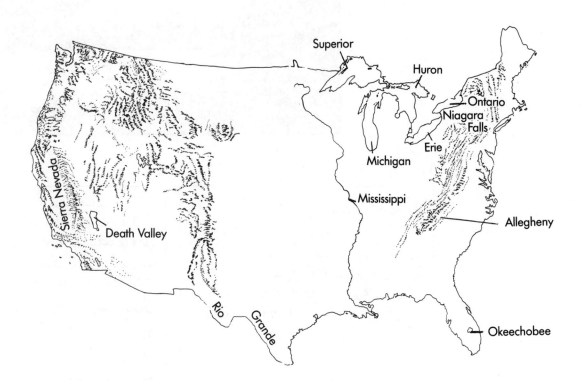

1. The Mississippi is a _river_.

2. Superior is a _____.

3. The Rio Grande is a _____.

4. Death Valley is a _____.

5. Niagara is a _____.

6. Okeechobee is a _____.

7. Sierra Nevada and Allegheny are names of _____.

8. Huron is a _____.

4 A POSTCARD. Look at the picture. Then put a check next to the correct message.

1.

> Dear Laura,
>   We spent yesterday fishing in this pond. and picking flowers in the meadows Wish you were here.
>   M.

2.

> Dear Laura,
>   Here I am in Kochel. yesterday we climbed to a snow-covered mountain peak. It's too cold to go boating on the lake, but it's nice to look at. See you soon.
>   M.

3.

> Dear Laura,
>   Have you ever seen such a fantastic waterfall? It looks just like this postcard. Too bad we can't go swimming. It would be nice to be at a lake. M.

4.

> Dear Laura,
>   Swimming in this river is great! The hills are covered with green grass and flowers - just like in the picture. I miss you.
>   M.

26 THE CAR

 1 AT THE GARAGE. A woman has brought her car in for a checkup. Listen and put a check next to the parts that need repair.

> **Artie's Auto Shop**
>
> ☑ brakes
> ☐ accelerator
> ☐ clutch
> ☐ gearshift
> ☐ battery
> ☐ air filter
> ☐ engine
> ☐ radiator
> ☐ tires
> ☐ turn signals
> ☐ temperature gauge
> ☐ fuel gauge
> ☐ speedometer
> ☐ windshield wiper

2 ODD MAN OUT. Cross out the word that does not belong.

1. ~~attendant~~   trunk   bumper   license plate

2. clutch   brake   turn signal   accelerator

3. ignition   windshield wiper   speedometer   heater

4. seat   sedan   convertible   station wagon

5. speedometer   fuel gauge   temperature gauge   gearshift

6. gas pump   air filter   hose   nozzle

3 **DIFFERENCES. Look at the two cars. Can you find eight differences between them?**

A

81658

B

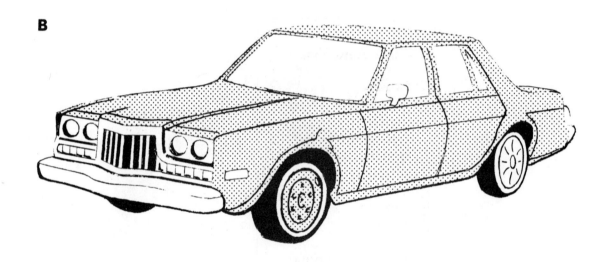

1. _Car A is white. Car B is gray._

2. _____

3. _____

4. _____

5. _____

6. _____

7. _____

8. _____

4 AT THE WHEEL. Complete the sentences.

1. If you want to know how fast
   you're going, you check the
   a. fuel gauge.
   b. speedometer.
   c. battery.

2. The car won't start. Maybe the
   _____ is dead.
   a. fuel gauge
   b. brake
   c. battery

3. If you want to make a right turn,
   you turn the _____ to the
   right.
   a. dashboard
   b. gearshift
   c. steering wheel

4. If you have a large family, you
   may need a
   a. convertible.
   b. station wagon.
   c. trunk.

5. If your fuel gauge says EMPTY,
   you should
   a. turn on the heater.
   b. go to a gas station.
   c. step harder on the accelerator.

6. If it's raining, you should turn
   on the
   a. windshield wipers.
   b. turn signal.
   c. ignition.

27 THE TRAIN, BUS & TAXI

1 **THE BUS OR THE TRAIN? A woman wants to travel from New York City to Providence, Rhode Island. She is making some phone calls to get information. Listen to her conversations and complete her notes.**

	Bus	Train
Fare		$44
Length of trip		
Number of stops		
Number of departures		

Now fill in the blanks with <u>bus</u> or <u>train</u> and <u>more</u> or <u>less</u>. Then complete the last sentence.

The _train_ to Providence is _____ expensive than the
    1   2

_____. But the _____ trip takes _____ time than the
 3   4   5

_____ trip. The _____ stops _____ often than the _____.
 6   7   8   9

The _____ leaves _____ often than the _____. In my
    10   11   12

opinion, the _____ is _____ comfortable than the _____ . I
        13   14   15

would prefer to take the _____ because _____
           16

_____

_____

TRAVELING. Complete the sentences.

1. When you're traveling by bus, you shouldn't talk to the
   a. passengers.
   b. driver. *(circled)*
   c. porter.

2. If you're at the train station and you can't find your track, you should go to the
   a. platform.
   b. passenger car.
   c. information booth.

3. You tried to get a taxi, but the driver didn't stop for you because the
   a. off-duty sign was on.
   b. driver didn't have any passengers.
   c. radio call sign was off.

4. _____ does NOT give you information about time.
   a. A clock
   b. An arrival and departure board
   c. A radio call sign

5. You CAN'T get information about _____ in a train schedule.
   a. track numbers
   b. arrival times
   c. the number of trains per day

6. When you're in a taxi, you can put your suitcases
   a. in the trunk.
   b. in the luggage compartment.
   c. on the door handle.

3 **AT THE TRAIN STATION. Look at the arrival and departure board. Then answer the questions.**

ARRIVALS			DEPARTURES		
Time	From	Track	Time	Destination	Track
7:05	Pleasantville	6	7:15	Stanford	7
7:40	Smithtown	7	8:30	Utopia	5
8:02	Utopia	5	8:45	Springfield	1
8:15	Libertyville	4	9:00	New Bedford	3
9:00	Madison	8	9:35	Newkirk	2

1. How many tracks does this train station have? *Eight*

2. Where is the 8:30 train going? _____

3. Where is the 8:15 train coming from? _____

4. Which train arrives at track 4? _____

5. Which train departs from track 1? _____

6. What time does the train arrive on track 8? _____

28 ROUTES & ROAD SIGNS

1 **ON THE ROAD. A police officer has just stopped a driver. Listen and put a check next to the mistakes the driver made.**

```
┌─────────────────────────────────────────────────┐
│              Traffic Violations                  │
│                                                  │
│  ☐  driving without driver's license             │
│  ☑  driving faster than speed limit              │
│  ☐  crossing double yellow line                  │
│  ☐  driving through red light                    │
│  ☐  driving through stop sign                    │
│  ☐  turning right against no right turn sign     │
│  ☐  turning left against no left turn sign       │
│  ☐  making illegal U-turn                        │
└─────────────────────────────────────────────────┘
```

2 **MEMORY GAME. Study the picture. Then cover it with a piece of paper. Read the words in the box and put a check next to the ones that are in the picture.**

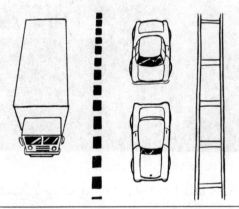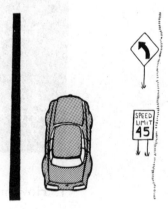

```
┌─────────────────────────────────────────────────┐
│      bridge              gray car(s)             │
│  ✓   broken line         black car(s)            │
│      solid line          45 speed limit sign     │
│      double lines        55 speed limit sign     │
│      divider             no U-turn sign          │
│      bus                 curve sign              │
│      truck               no right turn sign      │
│      white car(s)                                │
└─────────────────────────────────────────────────┘
```

3 ROAD TEST. Look at the signs and circle the correct answer.

1. If you see this sign, you must
   a. stop.
   b. drive at exactly 45 miles an hour.
   c. not drive faster than 45 miles an hour.

2. This sign is always
   a. green and white.
   b. yellow and black.
   c. red and white.

3. If you see this sign, you must
   a. turn left.
   b. turn right.
   c. not turn right.

4. This sign means that the road
   a. curves.
   b. goes up and down a hill.
   c. is slippery when it's wet.

5. This sign means that
   a. there is a shopping center nearby.
   b. there is a school nearby.
   c. you have to walk.

6. If the light turns green, you
   a. can go.
   b. must stop.
   c. should slow down.

7. This sign means that you can't make a
   a. left turn.
   b. right turn.
   c. U-turn.

8. This sign means
   a. a train may come.
   b. schoolchildren cross here.
   c. do not enter.

29 THE AIRPORT

 1 **FLYING. Listen to the announcements and circle the correct answer.**

1. Ms. López should
   a. show her ticket to the customs officer.
   b. go to the ticket counter.
   c. count her tickets.

2. Passengers for Flight 203 should
   a. pass through customs.
   b. show their boarding passes at the gate.
   c. take their carry-on luggage on board.

3. Mr. Uwinski should
   a. claim his baggage.
   b. go to the baggage claim area.
   c. go to the party in the waiting room.

4. This announcement was made
   a. at the gate.
   b. in the waiting room.
   c. on board the plane.

5. This announcement was made from
   a. the cockpit.
   b. the terminal.
   c. the control tower.

6. This announcement was made from
   a. the cockpit.
   b. the cabin.
   c. the control tower.

7. This announcement was probably
   made by
   a. the pilot.
   b. the co-pilot.
   c. a flight attendant.

8. This announcement was made
   a. in the waiting room.
   b. at customs.
   c. at the ticket counter.

2 TRUE OR FALSE? Read the sentences and write True or False. Correct the sentences that are false.

1. You usually buy your plane ticket <u>after</u> you get on board.

   False. You usually buy it before you get on board.

2. The pilot and co-pilot work in the <u>cabin</u>.

   _____

3. The arrival and departure board tells you the <u>gate numbers</u>.

   _____

4. The <u>flight attendant</u> looks in your luggage.

   _____

5. You select a seat <u>after</u> you board the plane.

   _____

6. A helicopter has a <u>tail and wings</u>.

   _____

7. The <u>flight attendant</u> watches the instrument panel.

   _____

8. Another word for *porter* is <u>*skycap*</u>.

   _____

9. Passengers put their carry-on luggage under the seat or in the <u>aisle</u>.

   _____

10. You have to show your passport to the <u>ticket agent</u>.

   _____

3 ODD MAN OUT. Cross out the word that does not belong.

1. ticket agent   security guard   ticket ~~counter~~   co-pilot

2. co-pilot   pilot   flight attendant   skycap

3. ticket   suitcase   boarding pass   passport

4. hangar   tail   wing   cabin

5. check-in counter   gate   waiting room   cockpit

6. armrest   tray   carousel   tray table

4 A POSTCARD. There are six mistakes in the postcard. Circle the incorrect words. Then write the correct forms below.

Dear Mom + Dad,

I'm sitting on (bord) my flight. I had to wait two hours in the waiting room before getting on this yet plane. I have an isle seat and the passenger next to me is very friendly. In about five minutes the flight atendent is going to serve lunch. The pylot said that we are going to arrive on time. I'll call you from Grandma's house.   Love, Jerry

1. _board_   4. _____

2. _____   5. _____

3. _____   6. _____

30 THE WATERFRONT THE BEACH

1 YOUR HOME AWAY FROM HOME. Listen to the radio ad and complete the sentences.

1. This is an ad for
   - a. a hotel.
   - b. an ocean liner.
   - c. a ferry.

2. The name of the hotel is
   - a. The Boardwalk.
   - b. The Starboard.
   - c. The Sand Castle.

3. It's located
   - a. on the harbor.
   - b. on the boardwalk.
   - c. at starboard.

4. The _____ that the announcer talks about is/are soft and white.
   - a. beach towels
   - b. sand
   - c. waves

5. The hotel has a private
   - a. swimming pool.
   - b. barge.
   - c. beach.

6. The ad does NOT mention
   - a. beach balls.
   - b. lounge chairs.
   - c. umbrellas.

7. The ad mentions a
   - a. dock worker.
   - b. longshoreman.
   - c. lifeguard.

8. The ad tells people to bring a
   - a. bathing suit.
   - b. beach blanket.
   - c. beach towel.

2 AT THE BEACH. Look at page 62 of your PHOTO DICTIONARY and answer the questions.

A. What are six places where you can sit at the beach?

1. _sand_   3. _____   5. _____

2. _____   4. _____   6. _____

B. What are two things that can protect you from the sun?

7. _____   8. _____

3 BEACH RULES. Complete the sign with the words in the box.

WELCOME TO SANIBEL BEACH
Rules and Regulations
1. Do not litter. Use the _trash cans_ .
2. Wear shoes when walking on the _____ .
3. Swim only when the _____ is on duty.
4. Take only five _____ per day.
5. _____ required!
6. Wear a _____ . The sun is strong.
7. Most important: Enjoy the _____ !

bathing suit	lifeguard
beach	seashells
boardwalk	trash cans
hat	

4 WHAT IS IT? Look at page 61 of your PHOTO DICTIONARY and fill in the blanks.

1. It's in the water and rhymes with clock. D Ⓞ C K

2. It's part of a ship and rhymes with now. __ __ Ⓞ

3. It's in the water and rhymes with large. __ Ⓞ __ __ __

4. It goes back and forth and rhymes with berry. Ⓞ __ __ __

5. It lifts heavy objects and rhymes with lane. __ Ⓞ __ __ __

6. It's on a boat and rhymes with neck. __ Ⓞ __ __

7. It carries cargo and rhymes with later. __ __ __ __ __ Ⓞ __

80

8. It's part of a ship and rhymes with <u>turn</u>.

___ (○) ___ ___

9. It means the same as the word in sentence 1 and rhymes with <u>near</u>.

___ ___ ___ (○) ___

10. It connects the boat to the pier and rhymes with <u>sign</u>.

___ ___ (○) ___

Now unscramble the letters in the circles.

___ ___ ___ ___ ___ ___ ___ ___ ___

5 COMPARING. Write sentences making comparisons.

1. (small) crane/buoy

   A buoy is smaller than a crane.

2. (long) boardwalk/pier

   _____

3. (big) ocean liner/ferry

   _____

4. (comfortable) lounge chair/lifeguard stand

   _____

5. (hard) sand/rock

   _____

6. (flat) barge/cargo ship

   _____

31 WINTER SPORTS WATER SPORTS

 1 **PLANNING A VACATION.** Julie Mills is talking to a travel agent. Listen and put a check in the correct boxes.

Terrific Trips Travel Agency
Questionnaire

☐ Water Sports   ☐ Winter Sports

  ☐ swimming   ☐ downhill skiing

    ☐ pool   ☐ cross country skiing

    ☐ ocean   ☐ skating

    ☐ lake   ☐ ice

  ☐ snorkeling   ☐ figure

  ☐ scuba diving   ☐ sledding

  ☐ fishing   ☐ snowmobiling

  ☐ surfing

  ☐ windsurfing

  ☐ waterskiing

  ☐ boating

    ☐ rowboat

    ☐ sailboat

    ☐ canoe

    ☐ kayak

  ☐ white water rafting

Now put a check next to the brochure the agent gave Julie.

1.

2.

3.

4. LAKESIDE BUNGALOWS

2 SPORTS TALK. Complete the sentences.

1. _____ is NOT a water sport.
   a. Sledding
   b. Canoeing
   c. Surfing

2. A canoeist uses
   a. an oar.
   b. a paddle.
   c. a surfboard.

3. A sailboat has a
   a. mast.
   b. towrope.
   c. pole.

4. A _____ makes the most noise.
   a. rowboat
   b. canoe
   c. motorboat

5. A water-skier holds on to
   a. an oar.
   b. a pole.
   c. a towrope.

6. You can go _____ in a lake.
   a. white water rafting
   b. fishing
   c. surfing

7. _____ does not require a helmet.
   a. Kayaking
   b. Bobsledding
   c. Diving

8. A _____ follows a trail.
   a. cross country skier
   b. swimmer
   c. figure skater

3 ODD MAN OUT. Cross out the word that does not belong.

1. swimmer   kayaker   skier   ~~mask~~
2. surfer   rower   skater   swimmer
3. diver   rower   canoeist   kayaker
4. surf   rapids   sail   swimming pool
5. air tank   mast   wet suit   helmet
6. snowmobile   rowboat   canoe   raft
7. ski   skate   boot   helmet
8. sail   mast   rower   oar

4 **WHAT GOES TOGETHER? Complete the analogies.**

1. skate:skater = ski:_skier_

2. ice:skater = _____ :swimmer

3. oar:_____ = paddle:canoe

4. _____ :white water rafting = wet suit:scuba diving

5. surfing:_____ = sledding:sled

6. raft:rapids = surfboard:_____

5 **COMPARING. Write sentences making comparisons.**

1. (deep) a swimming pool/the ocean

    The ocean is deeper than a swimming pool.

2. (exciting) rowing/white water rafting

    _____

3. (fast) bobsledding/snowmobiling

    _____

4. (difficult) snorkeling/scuba diving

    _____

5. (interesting) ice skating/figure skating

    _____

6. (cold) water skiing/cross country skiing

    _____

7. (dangerous) downhill skiing/cross country skiing

    _____

8. (soft) helmet/ski cap

    _____

32 SPECTATOR SPORTS OTHER SPORTS

1 **A FULL DAY.** Two campers are talking about the day's activities. Listen and complete the schedule.

Camp Caponga Schedule of Activities
Monday, August 11

8:00 *breakfast*

9:00 _____

10:00 _____

11:00 _____

12:00 *lunch*

2:00 _____

3:00 _____

5:00 _____

6:00 *dinner*

7:00 _____

2 **DOES IT BELONG THERE?** Cross out the names of people or things you usually **DON'T** find on a baseball diamond.

foul line	helmet	pitcher
umpire	tent	batter
~~quarterback~~	coach	glove
referee	first base	stirrup

3 **SPORTS QUESTIONNAIRE. Which sports have you participated in? Put a check under Participant. Which sports have you watched? Put a check under Spectator. Which would you like to learn?**

	Participant	Spectator	Would Like to Learn
1. archery			
2. baseball			
3. bowling			
4. boxing			
5. cycling			
6. football			
7. golf			
8. horse racing			
9. karate			
10. rollerskating			
11. tennis			
12. volleyball			
13. basketball			
14. soccer			
15. ping pong			

4 **SPEAKING OF SPORTS. Read the conversations. Then look at the schedule in Exercise 1 and decide what sport the people are talking about.**

1. A: Should I meet you on the green?

   B: Yes, and don't forget the balls. _golf_

2. A: Who moved the target?

   B: I did. _____

3. A: Do we need backpacks?

   B: Of course. And bring your map too. _____

4. A: I hope I can knock down that last pin.

   B: Just throw the ball carefully. _____

5. A: I can't get the ball over the net.

   B: Try hitting it with both hands. _____

6. A: If you don't use a saddle, you'll fall off.

   B: I guess you're right. _____

5 WHAT DO THEY HAVE IN COMMON? Write a sentence telling what the people or things have in common.

1. wrestler and boxer

   A wrestler and boxer fight.

2. tennis and squash

   _____

3. tennis and volleyball

   _____

4. referee and umpire

   _____

5. shin guard and helmet

   _____

6. bat and golf club

   _____

7. soccer and football

   _____

8. jogger and runner

   _____

9. volleyball and tennis

   _____

10. bowling and squash

    _____

33 | ENTERTAINMENT MUSICAL INSTRUMENTS

1 **THE TOP TEN.** Listen to the radio program and write the correct number next to this week's top ten songs.

TOP TEN HITS

I'm Just an Actress with You	_____	You Are My Spotlight	_____
The Audience Has Gone Home	_____	On Stage with You	_____
Blue Billboard	_____	Heart Strings	_____
Dark Drums	_____	Winter Woodwinds	_____
Tell It to the Trombone	_____	Meet Me under the Marquee	_____
Ballet Blues	_____	The Red Flute	_____
Cymbal of Love	_____	Bad Brass	_____

---

2 **A MUSICAL PUZZLE.** Look at page 70 of your **PHOTO DICTIONARY** and fill in the blanks.

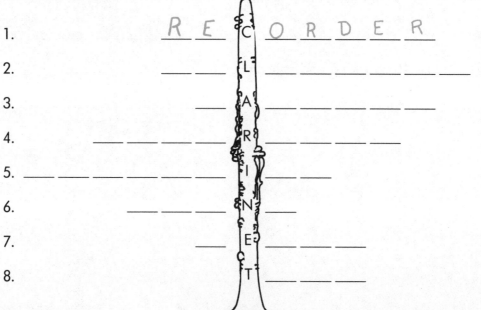

1. R E C O R D E R

2. _____ _____ _____ L _____ _____ _____

3. _____ _____ A _____ _____ _____

4. _____ _____ _____ R _____

5. _____ _____ _____ _____ I _____ _____ _____

6. _____ _____ N _____ _____

7. _____ _____ E _____ _____

8. _____ _____ T _____ _____

Now put the nine instruments into the correct category.

Strings	Brass	Woodwinds	Percussion	Other
_____	_____	*Clarinet*	_____	_____
_____	_____	_____	_____	_____
_____	_____	_____	_____	_____

3 THAT'S ENTERTAINMENT! Complete the sentences.

1. A large group of people playing musical instruments together is called
   a. an orchestra.
   b. an opera.
   c. a chorus.

2. Another word for <u>singer</u> is
   a. vocalist.
   b. chorus.
   c. opera.

3. A _____ is lit by footlights and spotlights.
   a. billboard
   b. marquee
   c. stage

4. An orchestra is led by
   a. a podium.
   b. an actor.
   c. a conductor.

5. A _____ is played with a bow.
   a. flute
   b. trombone
   c. bass

6. _____ is in the same musical family as a clarinet.
   a. An oboe
   b. A tuba
   c. A guitar

7. A drum is in the same musical family as a
   a. cymbal
   b. trumpet
   c. clarinet

8. A _____ is NOT played by blowing air into it.
   a. harmonica
   b. drum
   c. trumpet

9. A _____ does NOT have strings.
   a. guitar
   b. cymbal
   c. violin

4   **WEEKEND PLANS. Complete the conversation with the words in the box.**

actors	cello
audience	entertainment
ballerina	instrument
ballet	stage
ballet dancers	theater

SHARON: I want to do something different for

entertainment next weekend. Any ideas?
1

JIM: Well, have you ever been to a _____?
2

SHARON: Yes. I went last month, and the dancing was wonderful. One

_____ was especially good. She danced
3

to some beautiful _____ music.
4

JIM: Oh, that's my favorite _____.
5

SHARON: I like it too.

JIM: _____ have to be good
6

_____ too. That's one of the things I like
7

about it.

SHARON: Yes, it really does combine music, dance and

_____.
8

JIM: And I really like the people who go to the ballet. The

_____ is usually very enthusiastic.

SHARON: Do you think I can still get tickets for next weekend?

JIM: Yes, I think so. The last time I went I bought a ticket only a week in

advance and got a very good seat just five rows from the

_____.
10

34 THE ZOO & PETS

1 **WHAT'S THAT? A mother and son are at the zoo. Listen and choose the animals they're looking at.**

1. a. zebra
   b. camel
   c. giraffe

2. a. camel
   b. kangaroo
   c. elephant

3. a. lion
   b. polar bear
   c. elephant

4. a. rhinoceros
   b. deer
   c. bison

5. a. koala
   b. polar bear
   c. leopard

6. a. buffalo
   b. fox
   c. leopard

7. a. tiger
   b. leopard
   c. zebra

8. a. gorilla
   b. monkey
   c. raccoon

9. a. camel
   b. kangaroo
   c. elephant

10. a. deer
    b. bison
    c. rhinoceros

2 **TRUE OR FALSE? Read the sentences and write True or False. Correct the sentences that are false.**

1. A polar bear lives in a hot climate.

   False. A polar bear lives in a cold climate.

2. A llama has the longest neck of all the animals at the zoo.

   _____

3. You can see elephants at the zoo.

   _____

4. You can keep goldfish in a bowl.

   _____

3 AN ANIMAL FAMILY. Look at the pictures and write the names of the animals.

1. _____   2. _____

Now write the names of three things that these two animals have in common.

3. _____   4. _____   5. _____

Now compare the two animals.

6. (small) _____

7. (strong) _____

8. (dangerous) _____

4 WHAT IS IT? Fill in the blanks.

1. It's a part of an animal and rhymes with <u>sail</u>.

2. It's on a leopard and rhymes with <u>hot</u>.

3. It's part of an animal and rhymes with <u>couch</u>.

4. It's an animal that rhymes with <u>socks</u>.

5. It has antlers and rhymes with <u>pier</u>.

6. It's on a lion and rhymes with <u>rain</u>.

7. It's an animal that rhymes with <u>hair</u>.

8. It's part of an animal and rhymes with <u>corn</u>.

T A (I) L

Now unscramble the letters in the circles.

___ ___ ___ ___ ___ ___ ___ ___ ___

35 THE FARM
FISH & SEA ANIMALS

1 WHAT'S THAT? A father and daughter are at the aquarium. Listen and choose the sea animals they're looking at.

1. a. lobster
   b. eel
   c. crab

2. a. shark
   b. walrus
   c. whale

3. a. clams
   b. crabs
   c. mussels

4. a. turtle
   b. octopus
   c. crab

5. a. shark
   b. walrus
   c. dolphin

6. a. starfish
   b. lobster
   c. octopus

7. a. shark
   b. sunfish
   c. lobster

8. a. shark
   b. seal
   c. angelfish

2 ON THE FARM. Match the words in column A with the definitions in column B.

A	B
1. __d__ barn	a. a baby cow
2. ____ furrow	b. a long narrow track, especially one cut by a plow in farming
3. ____ combine	c. a plant or plant product such as grain, fruit or vegetable grown by a farmer
4. ____ calf	d. a building for storing crops and food for animals, or for keeping animals in
5. ____ crop	e. a wall made of wood or wire, dividing two areas of land
6. ____ fence	f. a machine that harvests wheat

3 **SCRAMBLED WORDS. Unscramble the words in the box. Then use them to complete the sentences.**

ganelsifh _angelfish_	dik _____
ulbl _____	eman _____
tuspooc _____	almc _____
lee _____	rahks _____

1. A horse has a _mane_ .

2. A baby goat is called a(n) _____ .

3. A cow is female, and a(n) _____ is male.

4. The _____ is a dangerous fish.

5. A(n) _____ looks like a snake.

6. A(n) _____ looks like a small tortoise.

7. A(n) _____ has stripes.

8. A(n) _____ has tentacles.

4 **A LETTER HOME. A 10-year-old girl is visiting a farm for the first time. There are eight incorrect facts in her letter. Cross out the mistakes and correct them.**

Dear Mom and Dad,

Today was a good day here at the farm. I
got up really early when I heard the ~~chicken~~ rooster
crow. Then I helped milk the bulls and
collect the sheeps eggs in the farmhouse. Before
lunch I rode the tractor with the farmer and
picked tomatoes in the wheat field. This summer
has been very dry and so they use a combine
to water the fields. In the afternoon I
watched the sheep with their baby kids.
Now I'm in the barn with the rest of the
family watching TV in the kitchen.
I'll write again soon.
        Love and Kisses,
        Mary

BIRDS
INSECTS & RODENTS

1   A NATURE WATCH. A woman is looking through a pair of field glasses. Listen and choose the things she sees.

3. a. swan
    b. swallow
    c. eagle

6. a. pelican
    b. stork
    c. cockatoo

1. a. ostrich
    b. swan
    c. crane

4. a. crow
    b. pigeon
    c. eagle

7. a. mouse
    b. rat
    c. squirrel

2. a. robin
    b. blue jay
    c. cockatoo

5. a. hummingbird
    b. robin
    c. stork

8. a. squirrel
    b. chipmunk
    c. mouse

2   COMPARING. Write sentences making comparisons.

1. (big) peacock/swallow/swan

   A swan is bigger than a swallow, but a peacock is biggest of all.

2. (small) duckling/duck/swan

   _____

   _____

3. (pretty) ladybug/butterfly/spider

   _____

   _____

95

3 DESCRIPTIONS. Match the words in column A with the descriptions in column B.

A		B
1. _C_ ant		a. It's long with many legs, and turns into a butterfly.
2. ____ spider		b. It spins a web to catch other insects.
3. ____ dragonfly		c. It's small and can't fly.
4. ____ butterfly		d. It makes honey.
5. ____ ladybug		e. It has a long body and four wings.
6. ____ bee		f. It bites people.
7. ____ caterpillar		g. It's small, round and red with black dots.
8. ____ mosquito		h. It has large, beautifully colored wings.

4 INSECT INDENTIFICATION. Look at the pictures and write the names of the insects.

1. ____bee____

2. _____

3. _____

4. _____

5. _____

6. _____

7. _____

8. _____

SPACE
THE MILITARY

1 **A SCIENCE LESSON.** Professor Latham is talking about space. Listen and choose the things he's describing.

1. a. Earth
   b. the Moon
   (c.) a galaxy

2. a. Earth
   b. the Moon
   c. Saturn

3. a. Earth
   b. the Moon
   c. the Sun

4. a. Earth
   b. the Moon
   c. Saturn

5. a. Earth
   b. the Moon
   c. Saturn

2 **OUR GALAXY.** Complete the paragraph with the words in the box.

astronauts	planet(s)
Earth	space
flag	stars
galaxy	Sun
Moon	

Our ____*Galaxy*____
                1

We live on the planet _____. There are eight other
                                    2

_____ in our galaxy. A _____ consists of
        3   4

millions and millions of _____. The Earth revolves around
                                5

one of these stars. We call it the _____. The
                                        6

_____, which we can see at night, moves around the Earth
        7

every 28 days. In 1969 two _____ from the United States
                                8

landed on the moon and put their country's _____ on it.
                                                9

_____ continues to be explored.
        10

3 NEIGHBORS IN SPACE. Our solar system consists of the Sun and nine planets. Look at the diagram and read the information in the chart. Then answer the questions.

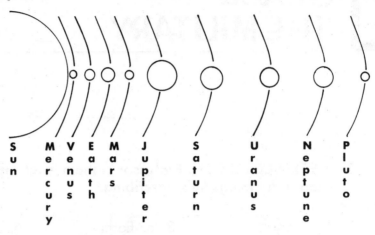

Planet	Distance from Sun (in millions of miles)	Year		Diameter (in miles)
Mercury	36	88	days	3,000
Venus	67	224–7	days	7,700
Earth	93	365	days	7,927
Mars	141.5	687	days	4,220
Jupiter	483	11.9	years	88,700
Saturn	886	29.5	years	75,100
Uranus	1,783	84	years	29,700
Neptune	2,793	164.8	years	31,000
Pluto	3,666	247.7	years	4,000?

1. Which planet is closest to the Sun? _Mercury_

2. Which planet is closest to Earth? _____

3. Which planet is farthest from the Sun? _____

4. Which planet is the fifth in order of distance from the Sun?

   _____

5. Which planet is closest in size to Earth? _____

6. Which planet is the largest? _____

7. Which planet is the smallest? _____

8. Which planet is colder, Jupiter or Mars? Why? _____

   _____

9. Which planet has the longest "year"? _____

10. Which planet has a longer "year," Mercury or Saturn? _____

4 FIGHTING WORDS. Complete the sentences.

1. _____ is in the army.
   a. A sailor
   b. An astronaut
   c. A pilot
   (d.) A soldier

2. _____ is NOT in the military.
   a. A sailor
   b. An astronaut
   c. A marine
   d. A soldier

3. A soldier wears
   a. a space suit.
   b. a parachute.
   c. fatigues.
   d. rifles.

4. It is sometimes difficult to see a soldier because of
   a. camouflage.
   b. jeeps.
   c. fatigues.
   d. cannons.

5. A _____ is NOT a weapon.
   a. bayonet
   b. rifle
   c. machine gun
   d. jeep

6. A _____ is NOT a vehicle.
   a. helicopter
   b. tank
   c. cannon
   d. submarine

7. If you jump out of a plane, you need a
   a. rifle.
   b. booster rocket.
   c. parachute.
   d. flag.

8. A fighter plane drops
   a. cannons.
   b. bombs.
   c. destroyers.
   d. bayonets.

9. A boat that can travel under water is called
   a. a submarine
   b. a battleship
   c. a destroyer
   d. an aircraft carrier

10. A battleship uses _____ to look for other ships.
    a. cannons
    b. parachutists
    c. a radar antenna
    d. a satellite

11. _____ fight on the land and on the sea.
    a. Soldiers
    b. Pilots
    c. Sailors
    d. Marines

12. A destroyer is a kind of
    a. plane.
    b. ship.
    c. cannon.
    d. soldier.

38 HOBBIES & GAMES SEWING & SUNDRIES

1 WHAT ARE THEY DOING? Listen and circle the correct answer.

1. What is the woman going to do?
   a. Write a letter.
   b. Wrap a box.
   c. Play cards.

2. What are the man and woman going to do?
   a. Play a game.
   b. Buy a camera.
   c. Sew.

3. What are the man and woman doing?
   a. Playing Scrabble®.
   b. Painting.
   c. Bird watching.

4. What does the man give the woman?
   a. A ribbon.
   b. A button.
   c. A compass.

5. What does the woman give the man?
   a. A protractor.
   b. A pair of scissors.
   c. A needle.

6. What is the woman's hobby?
   a. Stamp collecting.
   b. Astronomy.
   c. Coin collecting.

7. What is the woman looking through?
   a. A magnifying glass.
   b. A telescope.
   c. A camera.

8. What is the man's hobby?
   a. Photography.
   b. Woodworking.
   c. Weaving.

2 ORDERING. A woman wants to knit a sweater for her friend's birthday, and she has to follow six steps. Put the steps in the correct order.

____ knit sweater

____ put tissue paper in box

____ cover box with wrapping paper

____ put sweater in box

____ put bow on box

_1_ buy yarn

3 A CROSSWORD PUZZLE. Complete the puzzle.

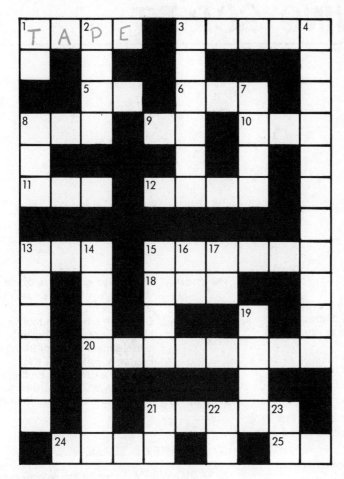

15 You need it for 4 Down.

18 First number

20 A board game

21 A library is full of them.

24 Not *there*

25 You and I

Down

1 ____ the left of

2 You can find them in a cushion.

3 A kind of pin

4 A hobby

7 Not *that*

8 It's made of ribbon.

13 Used to close clothes

14 You wear it on your middle finger.

15 Part of a collection

16 Do you have ____ eraser?

17 I

19 ____ and eye

21 The *Am, are, is* verb

22 Glass ____ water

23 Opposite of N.E. (Northeast)

Across

1 ____ measure

3 Part of a collection

5 The opposite of *yes*

6 The opposite of *thin*

8 A kind of transportation

9 Not *she*

10 You can knit this for your head.

11 The opposite of *dry*

12 You see with them.

13 Used in baseball

LISTENING SCRIPT

1 NUMBERS • TIME

1 THE KENTUCKY DERBY. The Kentucky Derby is the most famous horse race in the United States. Listen and write the positions of the horses as they run around the track.

ANNOUNCER: They're off! At the start, it's Lucky Lady first, Prince Charming second, Fast Buck third and Mad Hatter fourth.

At the first turn, it's Prince Charming first, Lucky Lady second, Fast Buck third and Mad Hatter fourth.

On the back stretch, Mad Hatter moves up to second place with Lucky Lady dropping back to third position. Prince Charming is still first and Fast Buck is fourth.

At the far turn, it's still Prince Charming first, Mad Hatter second, while Fast Buck moves ahead of Lucky Lady. So, Fast Buck is third and Lucky Lady is fourth.

In the final stretch, Fast Buck moves up and is now in second place with Prince Charming still first. Mad Hatter is third and Lucky Lady is fourth.

At the finish, Fast Buck just passes Prince Charming. So, its Fast Buck—first, Prince Charming—second, Mad Hatter—third and Lucky Lady—fourth.

2 CALENDAR • HOLIDAYS

1 MAKING AN APPOINTMENT. Mrs. Rivera is making an appointment with Dr. Becker's office. Listen and fill in the blanks.

RECEPTIONIST: Hello. Dr. Becker's office.

MRS. RIVERA: Hello. This is Mrs. Rivera. I'd like to make an appointment with Dr. Becker.

RECEPTIONIST: Let's see. . . . Dr. Becker can see you at two o'clock on Tuesday, January 26th.

MRS. RIVERA: I'm sorry, I can't make it on Tuesday. How about Wednesday the 27th?

RECEPTIONIST: Dr. Becker isn't in the office on Wednesday. How about Friday? That's January 29th.

MRS. RIVERA: Can I see him in the morning on Friday?

RECEPTIONIST: No, I'm sorry. He's busy then. The first appointment in the morning is Monday, February 1st at 8:00 A.M.

MRS. RIVERA: Oh, that's great. I'll be there on Monday the 1st at 8:00 A.M. Thank you.

RECEPTIONIST: You're welcome, Mrs. Rivera. See you then.

3 WEATHER & SEASONS

1 RADIO WQRV. Listen to the weather report and fill in the blanks.

ANNOUNCER: Good morning. This is Radio WQRV with the weather forecast for the Boston area for Friday, March 20th. The temperature at 7:00 A.M. is 32 degrees Fahrenheit and 0 degrees Celsius. The sky is clear and it's sunny. Afternoon temperatures will be around 40 degrees Fahrenheit, 3 degrees Celsius. Tonight will be cloudy and cold with temperatures dropping below freezing.

On Saturday, March 21st, it will be windy and stormy. Snow will develop in the late morning. Be careful driving. It may be foggy, and some roads will be icy.

On Sunday it will become warmer with temperatures rising into the high 40s. The forecast for next week shows warmer weather with highs in the 50s. It looks like winter is coming to an end and spring will soon be here.

4 SHAPES & MEASUREMENTS

1 A MYSTERY DRAWING. Listen and follow the directions.

In the center of the page, between points A and B, draw two one-inch circles side by side and about one inch apart.

Between the two circles and about one-half inch below them, draw an isosceles triangle with a one-inch base. One inch below the triangle, draw a small spiral. Then draw one large circle of about three and one-half inches in diameter around the two circles, triangle and spiral.

Now draw a half-inch square, touching the outer circumference of the large circle, near point B.

Draw another half-inch square directly opposite the first square. This square should also be touching the outer circumference of the circle.

Then at the bottom of the large circle, draw two parallel lines, about two inches apart, toward the bottom of the page.

Now you have completed the drawing.

5 MONEY & BANKING

1 THE JEFFERSON BANK. Listen to the radio ad for the Jefferson Bank. Then read the sentences and write True or False.

ANNOUNCER: The Jefferson Bank wants to be your bank. We offer many credit cards, including Visa and MasterCard, at no charge. You can get checkbooks of any color with your name on each check. You'll also receive a free check register with your checks. Get free traveler's checks and money orders from our tellers. Our computer does your monthly statement showing your deposits and withdrawals. Keep your important papers in our large vaults. Remember, at the Jefferson Bank you can use the cash machines twenty-four hours a day, seven days a week. We welcome new accounts, large or small. You can start an account with us with only five dollars. The Jefferson Bank wants to be your bank.

6 THE WORLD • THE UNITED STATES • CANADA

1 WORLD WIDE TOURS. Listen to the radio ad for World Wide Tours. On the map, write the names of the countries and oceans you hear.

ANNOUNCER: World wide tours offers you the best vacation to South America. We leave Saturday at 7:00 A.M. and fly to Lima, Peru on the Pacific Ocean. On Sunday, we'll visit the famous churches and museums of Lima. On Monday we'll fly to Cuzco and Machu Picchu to see the ancient Inca ruins. The next day we'll fly east to La Paz, Bolivia. On Wednesday we'll go south to Buenos Aires, Argentina. We'll stay at a large ranch and see the famous cowboys herd cattle. On Thursday we'll fly to Rio de Janeiro, Brazil, where we'll visit the beautiful beaches of Ipanema and Copacabana on the Atlantic Ocean. Friday is a free day in Rio. On Saturday we'll fly home.

This wonderful vacation is yours for only $675.

7 THE CITY

1 RADIO WQRV. Listen to the traffic report and put a check next to the picture that shows what people in Meadville should do today.

ANNOUNCER: Good morning. This is Radio WQRV with the latest traffic report. The bus strike in Meadville continues. There are no buses in the city today. The subways are running, and there will be extra taxis in the city during the strike. If you're riding your bicycle today, use the bus lanes. Be sure you ride in the same direction as the cars. Many people will be driving into the city today. Drivers, please don't block the crosswalks. Be careful of pedestrians. Pedestrians, cross only at the crosswalks. For more information stay tuned to WQRV for our next report at 7:30. Back to you, Jack . . . (fade out)

8 THE SUPERMARKET • FRUIT • VEGETABLES

1 A SHOPPING LIST. Juan and María are going to the supermarket. Listen and put a check next to the items they're going to buy.

MARÍA: Juan, we have to go to the supermarket. We need food for the week.
JUAN: OK. What do we need? I'll make a list.
MARÍA: We need meat. Let's get a roast, some pork chops and a chicken.
JUAN: OK. Roast, pork chops, chicken. How about a steak?
MARÍA: Fine.
JUAN: Do we need milk?
MARÍA: Yes, we need two cartons of milk. We also need eggs, butter and cheese.
JUAN: How about some yogurt?
MARÍA: Oh no! I hate yogurt. Don't get that.
JUAN: (laughs) OK, I won't. Do we need any frozen orange juice?
MARÍA: Yes, we do. And we need frozen vegetables too.
JUAN: Do we need any tuna fish?
MARÍA: That's a good idea. Write down three cans of tuna fish. We also need five cans of soup.
JUAN: OK. That's three cans of tuna and five cans of soup.
MARÍA: We also need bread and crackers.
JUAN: OK. What about fruit and vegetables?
MARÍA: Let's get a head of lettuce, a bunch of celery and a pound of potatoes.
JUAN: OK.
MARÍA: Don't get any cabbage or turnips.
JUAN: (laughs) OK I won't put them on the list. I know you hate them.
MARÍA: But I love fruit, so write down a bunch of grapes, a pound of bananas and a box of strawberries.
JUAN: Fine. Let's get a mango too.
MARÍA: Great. Let's go to the store now. I'm getting hungry.

9 THE MENU • FAST FOODS & SNACKS

1 AT A RESTAURANT. Lisa and Peter are at a restaurant. Listen and write what they order for dinner.

WAITER:	Hi, I'm Walter. I'm your waiter tonight.
LISA:	Hi, Walter.
WAITER:	The specialities of the day are roast beef with carrots and green beans and fresh fish with a baked potato and broccoli.
PETER:	What would you like, Lisa?
LISA:	I'd like pork chops and carrots.
PETER:	And I'll have steak and a baked potato.
WAITER:	Would you like an appetizer?
LISA:	I'll have a fruit cup.
PETER:	I'd like a shrimp cocktail.
WAITER:	You can also have soup or a salad.
LISA:	Salad, please.
PETER:	I'd like soup, please.
WAITER:	For dessert, I'd recommend the chocolate cake.
LISA:	Cake is too fattening. I'll have jello.
PETER:	Do you have apple pie?
WAITER:	No, we don't, but we have chocolate pie and cherry pie.
PETER:	I'll have cherry pie, please.
WAITER:	Coffee or tea?
LISA:	I'll have coffee.
PETER:	Tea for me.
WAITER:	OK. Your dinner will be ready soon.
LISA AND PETER:	Thanks, Walter.

10 THE POST OFFICE • THE OFFICE

1 AT THE OFFICE. Agnes is asking her secretary, Mary, to do some things for her. Listen and answer the questions.

AGNES:	Mary, please go to the post office and mail this package to Mr. Arnold Pérez at the Ames Company. Send it express mail.
MARY:	The Ames Company? Let's see. I think I have their new address in my Rolodex. Here it is. It's 69 Bay State Road, Boston, MA 02187.
AGNES:	That's right. Also send this letter to Ms. Joan Miller in California. Do you have her address?
MARY:	Yes, she's at 2341 Broad Street, San Diego, California 92093.
AGNES:	Please send the letter certified mail and get a return receipt.
MARY:	OK. Do you need anything else at the post office?
AGNES:	Yes, get two rolls of stamps and one book of stamps. Then after you finish at the post office, please go next door to the stationery store and get ten file folders, six message pads, five pens and eight pencils.
MARY:	I'll go right now.
AGNES:	That's great. Thanks, Mary.

11 THE BODY • ACTION AT THE GYM

1 WAKE UP YOUR BODY. Joan Fander of Radio WQRV is teaching an exercise class. Look at the pictures. Then listen and put a check next to the pictures that show the exercises.

JOAN:	Good morning. I'm Joan Fander at Radio WQRV, with the program WAKE UP YOUR BODY. Now, stand up and let's do our exercises.

Exercise 1: Lift your right arm above your head and stretch 1, 2, 3, 4. Now put your right arm down at your side.

Exercise 2: Lift your left arm above your head and stretch 1, 2, 3, 4. Now put your left arm down at your side.

Exercise 3: Lift both arms above your head and stretch 1, 2, 3, 4. Keep stretching 5, 6, 7, 8. Stretch, stretch, stretch. Good. Now let's do . . .

Exercise 4: Put both arms down toward your toes. Try to reach your toes 1, 2, 3, 4. Don't bend your knees 5, 6, 7, 8. Good, very good. Now stand up straight and let's do . . .

Exercise 5: Put both hands on your waist *and* bend toward your left side 1, 2, 3, 4. *And* stand up straight 1, 2, 3, 4. Great!

Exercise 6: With both hands on your waist, bend toward your right side 1, 2, 3, 4. *And* stand up straight 1, 2, 3, 4. Good. Now take a deep breath. Next we'll do . . .

Exercise 7: Run in place to the count of 8. Left foot first 1, 2, 3, 4, 5, 6, 7, 8. Good. Stop. Take a deep breath. *And* . . .

Exercise 8: Hop on your left foot, 1, 2, 3, 4, 5, 6, 7, 8. Stop. Good. Doesn't your body feel great? That's all for today. This is Joan Fander for Radio WQRV. See you tomorrow!

12 COSMETICS & TOILETRIES • ACTION AT HOME

1 A MAKEUP LESSON. Cassandra Alexandra of Radio WQRV is giving some helpful hints for putting on makeup. Listen and write the numbers and the names of the cosmetics she talks about.

Welcome! I'm Cassandra Alexandra, and I'm going to give you a makeup lesson. Gentlemen, this show isn't only for the ladies. You should listen too, so you can help your girlfriends, wives and daughters look more beautiful. Now follow along with me.

Wash your face. Always begin with a clean face.

Number 1: Put some blush on your cheeks. Use only a little. We want you to have a natural look.

Number 2: Put on some eye shadow. Use the eye shadow on your upper eyelid and under your eyebrow.

Number 3: Use an eyebrow pencil very lightly on your eyebrow.

Number 4: Put some eyeliner on your lower eyelid. Draw a smooth line along the eyelid. You might want to put eyeliner on your upper lid too, close to your eyelashes.

Number 5: Put mascara on your lashes. This will make your lashes look long and lovely.

Number 6: Put on your lipstick. Be sure to follow the outline of your lips.

Now ladies, don't you feel beautiful?

And gentlemen, don't they look beautiful?

I'm Cassandra Alexandra of Radio WQRV. Until the next time . . . (fade out)

13 ACTION AT SCHOOL

1 IN THE CLASSROOM. Mrs. Rodríguez is talking to her class. Listen and match the students' names in column A with the pictures in column B.

MRS. RODRÍGUEZ: Good morning, class. We have a lot to do today. You'll all have to help. John, please erase everything on the blackboard. Jane, write the date on the board and Mary, you draw a circle. Steven, pick up the books and carry them to the front of the class. Lisa, don't tear up that paper. Put it in the wastepaper basket. Oh, you don't know where it is? Anne, please point to the wastepaper basket. Thanks. Beth, get some brushes so you can finish your painting. And Tim, please pick up the pens on the floor. Rick, begin reading page 55 in your book. And Laura, cut a piece of paper in half. Great. Now we can begin!

14 THE DOCTOR ● THE DENTIST

1 WHERE ARE THEY? Where do the conversations take place? Listen and put a check in the correct column.

NARRATOR: Number 1.
DOCTOR: You have a really bad cough. It's good that you came to see me.
PATIENT: Yeah, I feel just awful.

NARRATOR: Number 2.
DOCTOR: Now, open wide.
PATIENT: Is it going to hurt?
DOCTOR: Not with this shot of Novocain.

NARRATOR: Number 3.
DOCTOR: Where does it hurt?
PATIENT: On the left side, in the back.
DOCTOR: Uh-huh, I see. One of your fillings fell out.

NARRATOR: Number 4.
PATIENT: I've had a headache all week.
DOCTOR: Well, sit down on the examining table. I want to take your blood pressure.

NARRATOR: Number 5.
DOCTOR: Hmmm. I want to see if you're using your toothbrush correctly.
PATIENT: But . . . I brush after every meal and I floss once a day.

NARRATOR: Number 6.
PATIENT: Well, what do you think?
DOCTOR: The only way to correct that overbite is with braces.

NARRATOR: Number 7.
DOCTOR: I'm going to write you a prescription.
PATIENT: Is that for my cough?
DOCTOR: Yes. And you can take aspirin for your headache and fever.

NARRATOR: Number 8.
PATIENT: Do you think we can save the tooth?
DOCTOR: I'm not sure. We'll have to x-ray it.

15 OCCUPATIONS ● THE FAMILY ● EMOTIONS

1 María, Lisa and Kenji are high school students. They're talking about what they're going to do after graduation. Listen and fill in the blanks.

MARÍA Lisa, what are you going to do after graduation?
LISA: I'm going to be a secretary in my father's office. My father is very happy that I'll be working with him, but my mother is angry. She wants me to be a teacher. What are you going to do, Kenji?
KENJI: Me? Oh, I'm going to be a computer technician and make a lot of money. My father thinks it's a good idea, and he's really proud of me. My brother is an artist, and he doesn't make much money. Maybe I can help him. How about you, María? What are you going to do?
MARÍA: It's a problem. I don't know what I'm going to do, so I'm feeling very confused. My father wants me to be a nurse, my mother wants me to a teller in a bank and my brothers think I should be a journalist. I think I'm too shy to be a journalist. Oh, I don't know . . . maybe I'll be a teller.
KENJI: My cousin Rita is a teller, and she loves her job. She really likes working with people.
MARÍA: Well, sometimes I feel annoyed when I'm with people. Maybe I should be a veterinarian!
LISA & KENJI: Yes, María, maybe you should!

16 OPPOSITES

1 AT THE POLICE STATION. Mr. Prudente is very worried because his wife didn't come home from work today. He's talking to a police officer. Listen and put a check next to the correct picture.

POLICE OFFICER: Can you describe your wife, Mr. Prudente?
MR. PRUDENTE: Yes. She's tall and has dark brown hair and eyes.
POLICE OFFICER: Is her hair long or short?
MR. PRUDENTE: It's short.
POLICE OFFICER: Straight or curly?
MR. PRUDENTE: Curly.
POLICE OFFICER: OK. Can you remember what she was wearing when you last saw her?
MR. PRUDENTE: Yes. She had on a dark gray dress.
POLICE OFFICER: Do you remember anything else about the dress?
MR. PRUDENTE: Uh . . . no.
POLICE OFFICER: Well, what about her shoes?

MR. PRUDENTE:	She always wears low heels.
POLICE OFFICER:	Can you tell us anything else? Every bit of information can help us find your wife.
MR. PRUDENTE:	Well, her front teeth are a little crooked.
POLICE OFFICER:	OK. We'll send out this description right away.

17 MEN'S WEAR ● WOMEN'S WEAR

1 A DESIGNER'S ADVICE. A fashion designer is talking on a TV show. Listen and put a check next to the pictures that show the clothes he thinks men should wear this year.

MARY:	Good morning. I'm Mary Bart and my guest today is Harvey Blakely, the famous designer of men's wear. Welcome to the show, Harvey.
HARVEY:	Thanks, Mary. It's nice to be here.
MARY:	Tell us a little about what the well-dressed man should wear this year, Harvey.
HARVEY:	Sure, Mary. Well, men, for casual wear, you should wear a sport jacket. The jacket can be solid, plaid or checked, not striped or plaid. Striped and paisley sport jackets were popular last year, but this year your jacket must be solid, plaid or checked. Wear a light shirt— blue, white or tan. No dark shirts this year. By that I mean no red or black shirts. Your tie should be solid or striped. Don't wear a plaid or checked tie, please.
MARY:	What about jeans, Harvey?
HARVEY:	Oh, jeans are OK for very casual wear. In fact, they're great. But, please, no t-shirts this year. Wear a sport shirt—any color is fine. A sweater looks nice with jeans—you can wear it over your shirt if you want. But don't wear a vest. No vests with jeans.
MARY:	That makes sense to me. What are men wearing to the office, Harvey?
HARVEY:	The well-dressed businessman should wear a dark blue or gray suit. Either solid or striped is fine. No checked suits this year. Always wear a solid shirt and only light colors, please— white, yellow, blue. Never wear a checked or plaid shirt with a suit. Now for the tie—this year the well-dressed man is wearing striped or paisley ties. Yes, paisley is back but flowered and polka dot ties are out. Never, never wear a flowered or polka dot tie with a suit.
MARY:	Thanks, Harvey. That was very helpful. We have to break for a commercial. We'll be right back. (fade out)

18 MEN'S & WOMEN'S WEAR ● ACCESSORIES

1 THE SALE OF A LIFETIME! Listen to the radio ad for Lacey's Department Store and put a check next to the items that are on sale. Then write the sale price.

ANNOUNCER:	Lacey's Department Store is having a 100th-anniversary sale! Visit our shoe department. Women's slippers were $12.99, now on sale for only $6.99. Men's and women's sandals are now half price,

reduced from $29.99 to $14.99. And sneakers! Yesterday they were $16.99— buy them today for only $12.99!
Come to the women's department for great bargains on robes and nightgowns, regularly priced at $35.99, now just $30.99.

In the jewelry department you'll find items at half their regular price: watches for $15.99, earrings for $6.99 and silver cuff links for the incredible price of $29.99. Diamond rings start at the low price of $175.00!

Before you leave Lacey's, visit the accessory department. Handbags and briefcases are only $25.99, wallets and change purses are just $7.99.
So hurry to Lacey's today. You'll be glad you did. It's the sale of a lifetime!

19 HOUSING ● THE BACKYARD AND GARDEN

1 BUYING A HOUSE. Ginny and Bob Wilson want to buy a house. They're talking to a real-estate agent. Listen and put a check in the correct boxes.

AGENT:	So, how can I help you?
BOB:	We're looking for a house.
AGENT:	Well, let me ask you some questions, and then I can show you a house that's right for you. First, what kind of house would you like?
BOB:	We'd like a large ranch house.
AGENT:	OK. How many bedrooms do you want?
BOB:	Three bedrooms.
GINNY:	Well, I'd like four bedrooms. We want to have a lot of children.
AGENT:	No problem. Is a dining room important to you?
BOB:	It would be nice to have a dining room.
GINNY:	Yes, and I'd like a large kitchen too.
AGENT:	OK. How many bathrooms would you like?
BOB:	We'd like three bathrooms.
AGENT:	Fine. Let's think about the outside now. Is a garage important to you?
BOB:	Oh, yes. I'd like a garage.
AGENT:	Fine. How do you feel about a porch or patio?
BOB:	I don't care.
GINNY:	I'd love to have a patio in the backyard, with lots of grass.
BOB:	I'll agree to that only if you promise to mow the lawn.
GINNY:	OK, Bob, I promise.
AGENT:	Good. I'm glad you two agree. I think I have the perfect house for you. Look at the houses in these pictures. What do you think of this one?
BOB:	It's very nice.
AGENT:	Let's go and look at it right now.
GINNY:	Great!

20 THE LIVING ROOM ● THE DINING ROOM ● THE BEDROOM ● THE BATHROOM

1 WHERE ARE THEY? Where do the conversations take place? Listen and put a check in the correct column.

NARRATOR: Number 1
MAN: Are you finished setting the table?
WOMAN: Almost. I just have to put the centerpiece in the middle.

NARRATOR: Number 2.
WOMAN: This sofa is really comfortable.
MAN: Thanks. I bought it with the two club chairs last week.

NARRATOR: Number 3.
MAN: This quilt isn't warm enough.
WOMAN: Maybe we need the electric blanket tonight.

NARRATOR: Number 4.
MAN: Is there any more toothpaste?
WOMAN: I don't know. Look in the medicine cabinet.

NARRATOR: Number 5.
WOMAN: Have you seen my blue sweater?
MAN: Yes. It's in the top drawer of the chest.

NARRATOR: Number 6.
MAN: There's no more soap in the soap dish.
WOMAN: There's some here in the soap dispenser.

NARRATOR: Number 7.
WOMAN: Have you seen my PHOTO DICTIONARY?
MAN: You left it over there on the coffee table.

NARRATOR: Number 8.
MAN: Where should I put the wine glasses?
WOMAN: To the right of the water glasses.

21 THE KITCHEN • KITCHENWARE

1 IN THE KITCHEN. Manny and Laura are going to make some coffee. Listen and put a check next to the items they use.

MANNY: Do you want some coffee?
LAURA: Sure. Let me help you.
MANNY: Ok. My coffee maker is broken, so I have to use a pot to boil the water. The measuring cup is on the counter.
LAURA: I see it. And where do you keep the coffee?
MANNY: There's a can in the refrigerator. And you'll find measuring spoons in the cabinet drawer. I'll get two cups. Do you take milk in your coffee?
LAURA: No, I don't. I drink it black.
MANNY: I drink mine black too. What about sugar?
LAURA: No, no sugar.
MANNY: OK, then we don't need spoons. Oh, the water's boiling.

22 THE NURSERY • THE PLAYGROUND

1 WHAT'S ON SALE? Listen to the radio ad for the Toddlers and Tots store. Look at the pictures and cross out the incorrect information.

ANNOUNCER: This week Toddlers and Tots is having a sale on all nursery items. Playpens, usually costing $200.00 are on sale now for just $150.00. Choose a new baby carriage from three colors—red, blue or green—priced at just $75.00. Save $20.00 on strollers, on sale now for just $75.00. Buy a car seat, usually priced at $100.00, on sale now for only $75.00. Baby carriers in red, blue or yellow are just $25.00—if you buy one this week. Get a high chair, usually $75.00—this week only $55.00. And you can save on cribs too, selling for just $150.00. For these savings and more, come to Toddlers and Tots today.

23 THE LAUNDRY ROOM • TOOLS • CONSTRUCTION

1 WHAT'S HAPPENING? Listen and circle the correct answer.

NARRATOR: Number 1.
MAN: Where's the detergent?
WOMAN: It's on the washing machine.

NARRATOR: Number 2.
WOMAN: I can't find the clothespins.
MAN: They're on the floor next to the laundry basket.

NARRATOR: Number 3.
MAN: Have you seen my blue shirt?
WOMAN: Oh, I thought it was dirty.

NARRATOR: Number 4.
MAN: The living room carpet is really dirty. Where's the vacuum cleaner?
WOMAN: The vacuum cleaner is broken.

NARRATOR: Number 5.
MAN: It's raining.
WOMAN: I know. We'll have to dry the clothes inside.

NARRATOR: Number 6.
WOMAN: Why is it so dark in this room?
MAN: The light burned out. I'll go to the store.

NARRATOR: Number 7.
WOMAN: Hmmmm.
MAN: What's the matter?
WOMAN: The cord for the iron doesn't reach the socket.

NARRATOR: Number 8.
WOMAN: I can't get this nail out of the wall.
MAN: Here. Try this.

NARRATOR: Number 9.
MAN: It's going to take me hours to paint this room!
WOMAN: Why don't you use *this* instead of a brush?

NARRATOR: Number 10.
MAN: Do you have a tape measure?
WOMAN: No, but you can use this

24 ELECTRONICS

1 THE BIGGEST SAVINGS IN TOWN. Listen to the radio ad for Wild Willy's Electronics Shop. Look at the newspaper ad and put a check next to the items that are on sale.

ANNOUNCER: This weekend Wild Willy's is having its biggest sale ever. Save on VCRs normally priced at $349.95 now selling for just $229.95. And video cameras on sale for

$1088.00. Cassette decks are on sale for only $189. Choose from our large selection of compact discs—on sale for $12.99 each. And you can also save $10.00 on all AM/FM clock radios and cassette players. Buy your own telephone, on sale now for just $34.95. Electronic typewriters are marked down as low as $188.00. Yes! Come to Wild Willy's for the biggest savings in town. See your yellow pages for the location nearest you and save like you've never saved before!

25 LAND & WATER

1 WHERE ARE THEY? Listen and circle the correct answer.

NARRATOR: Number 1.
MAN: Are we almost there?
WOMAN: We have about a mile before we reach the peak.

NARRATOR: Number 2.
WOMAN: It's so cool and dark here.
MAN: Yes. And the trees are really beautiful.

NARRATOR: Number 3.
MAN: Don't step too near the edge!
WOMAN: Don't worry. I won't fall off.

NARRATOR: Number 4.
WOMAN: I'm really hot and thirsty.
MAN: Well, we won't find any water around here!

NARRATOR: Number 5.
MAN: What beautiful flowers!
WOMAN: Let's pick some and bring them back with us.

NARRATOR: Number 6.
WOMAN: Do you think we can swim to the other side?
MAN: Sure. It's not as big as a lake.

26 THE CAR

1 AT THE GARAGE. A woman has brought her car in for a checkup. Listen and put a check next to the parts that need repair.

WOMAN: So, have you looked at my car?
ARTIE: Yes, ma'am, I have. And a lot of things need repair. Your brakes, for example, need adjusting.
WOMAN: What about the accelerator?
ARTIE: The accelerator's fine and so is the clutch. But the gear shift needs repair.
WOMAN: Did you check the battery?
ARTIE: Yes. It's fine. But I have to clean the air filter.
WOMAN: What about the engine and radiator?
ARTIE: They're both in good working condition.
WOMAN: And the tires?
ARTIE: Well, your front tires are pretty low. They need to be changed.
WOMAN: OK. Did you check the turn signals?
ARTIE: Yes, and your left turn signal is broken.
WOMAN: Anything else?
ARTIE: Yes. Your temperature gauge isn't accurate. It needs adjusting.

WOMAN: And the fuel gauge?
ARTIE: The fuel gauge is fine, and so is the speedometer.
WOMAN: Is that all?
ARTIE: No. I checked your windshield wipers, and they need adjustment too.

27 THE TRAIN, BUS & TAXI

1 THE BUS OR THE TRAIN? A woman wants to travel from New York City to Providence, Rhode Island. She is making some phone calls to get information. Listen to her conversations and complete her notes.

CLERK: Longline Bus. Good morning.
WOMAN: Hello, can you tell me how much the bus fare is from New York City to Providence, Rhode Island?
CLERK: It's $44.00 round trip.
WOMAN: I see. And how long is the trip?
CLERK: About four hours.
WOMAN: Does the bus make many stops?
CLERK: It makes four stops before it arrives in Providence.
WOMAN: I see. And how often does the bus run?
CLERK: It leaves five times a day.
WOMAN: Thank you.

CLERK: Hello. Fast-Track Trains.
WOMAN: Oh, hello. I'd like to know the round-trip fare from New York City to Providence, Rhode Island.
CLERK: That's $56.00.
WOMAN: And how long is the trip?
CLERK: It takes 3 1/2 hours.
WOMAN: Does the train make many stops?
CLERK: Just two. One in New Haven and one in New London.
WOMAN: And how often does it run?
CLERK: It leaves three times a day.
WOMAN: Thank you.
CLERK: Thank you for calling Fast-Track.

28 ROUTES & ROAD SIGNS

1 ON THE ROAD. A police officer has just stopped a driver. Listen and put a check next to the mistakes the driver made.

OFFICER: Excuse me, sir. Can I see your driver's license?
MAN: Of course. Here it is. What seems to be the problem?
OFFICER: Well, first of all, you were driving 60 miles per hour and the speed limit is 55. You also crossed a double yellow line. And about a mile back, you drove right through a stop sign without stopping!
MAN: (incredulously) I didn't see a stop sign.
OFFICER: Well, it was there. And before you passed the stop sign, you turned left against a no left turn sign.
MAN: (even more incredulously) A no left turn sign? I didn't see one.
OFFICER: Well, it was there too. Here's your license and a ticket for all four traffic violations.

29 THE AIRPORT

1 FLYING. Listen to the announcements and circle the correct answer.

NARRATOR: Number 1.
WOMAN: Paging Ms. López. Mr. Wendy López. Please come to the ticket counter. Ms. Wendy López. Please come to the ticket counter.

NARRATOR: Number 2.
WOMAN: This is the last call for Flight 203. Last call for Flight 203. Passengers, please come to Gate 25 and have your boarding passes ready.

NARRATOR: Number 3.
WOMAN: Paging Mr. Uwinski. Mr. Richard Uwinski. Please meet your party at the baggage claim area.

NARRATOR: Number 4.
WOMAN: Attention, all passengers. Please make sure that your carry-on luggage is stored safely in the overhead compartments or under the seat in front of you and that your tray is in an upright position.

NARRATOR: Number 5.
MAN: This is your captain speaking. We are flying at an altitude of 35,000 feet. If you look out the windows on the left side of the plane, you'll be able to see the Atlantic Ocean.

NARRATOR: Number 6.
MAN: Flight 604, the runway is now cleared, and you are OKed for takeoff.

NARRATOR: Number 7.
WOMAN: We will be serving lunch in about ten minutes. Please put your tray tables down, and we will be with you shortly.

NARRATOR: Number 8.
MAN: Please have your passports and other documents ready.

30 THE WATER FRONT • THE BEACH

1 YOUR HOME AWAY FROM HOME. Listen to the radio ad and complete the sentences.

ANNOUNCER: Are you looking for the perfect hotel? Come to the Sand Castle. The Sand Castle is located directly on the boardwalk, just minutes away from the soft white sand of our beautiful private beach. Relax on our comfortable lounge chairs under our colorful umbrellas. Swim in the ocean. Our lifeguard is there to make your vacation enjoyable and safe. So, bring your bathing suit and leave all your troubles at home. This vacation, make the Sand Castle your home-away-from-home. For more information, call (805) 632-1785.

31 WATER SPORTS • WINTER SPORTS

1 PLANNING A VACATION. Julie Mills is talking to a travel agent. Listen and put a check in the correct boxes.

AGENT: So, how can I help you?
JULIE: Well, I want to go on vacation. I'd like to go to a place where I can participate in a lot of sports.
AGENT: I see. Well, let me ask you some questions. First of all, do you prefer water sports or winter sports?
JULIE: Water sports. I really want to go someplace warm.
AGENT: What kind of water sports do you like?
JULIE: I like to swim.
AGENT: Swimming. OK. Do you prefer a beach or a pool?
JULIE: Well, I love to dive, so I definitely want a swimming pool. But I also love the beach.
AGENT: OK. What about sports like snorkeling and scuba diving?
JULIE: Well, I've never gone snorkeling or scuba diving before. I think I'd be afraid of scuba diving, but I would like to try snorkeling.
AGENT: And what about fishing? Do you like fishing?
JULIE: No. I'm not interested in fishing.
AGENT: Do you have any interest in surfing?
JULIE: No, not really.
AGENT: And how about boating?
JULIE: Yes. I like some kinds of boating.
AGENT: What kinds?
JULIE: Sailing is my favorite.
AGENT: Have you ever tried white water rafting?
JULIE: No, and I don't really want to.
AGENT: OK. Why don't you look over this travel brochure and call me tomorrow.
JULIE: Great. Thanks a lot.

32 SPECTATOR SPORTS • OTHER SPORTS

1 A FULL DAY. Two campers are talking about the day's activities. Listen and complete the schedule.

CAMPER 1: What's on our schedule for today?
CAMPER 2: Well, we have breakfast at 8:00, as usual. Then at 9:00 we have archery.
CAMPER 1: How long does archery last?
CAMPER 2: An hour. Then we go to volleyball.
CAMPER 1: What happens after that?
CAMPER 2: Well, at 11:00 we go horseback riding for an hour before lunch at 12:00.
CAMPER 1: Then what?
CAMPER 2: Well, after lunch we have golf from 2:00 to 3:00. Then at 3:00 we go hiking for two hours. After that, we play tennis for an hour before dinner.
CAMPER 1: Is that it?
CAMPER 2: No. There's an evening activity too. At 7:00 we go bowling.
CAMPER 1: Sounds like a full day!

33 ENTERTAINMENT • MUSICAL INSTRUMENTS

1 THE TOP TEN. Listen to the radio program and write the correct numbers next to this week's top ten songs.

DISC JOCKEY: Good morning. This is Radio WQRV, and I'm Rockin' Robin with this week's top ten records. Starting with number 10, we have—for the second week in a row—*I'm Just an Actress with You*. Number 9 on our chart is *Dark Drums*. Number 8—*The Audience Has Gone Home*. For the third week in a row—hit number 7—*Winter Woodwinds*. Number 6 for this week—a song called *On Stage with You*. Number 5, a new hit called *Tell It to the Trombone*. Number 4 is *Bad Brass*. Moving to number 3 we have *Heart Strings*. And number 2 for the second week in a row is *Meet Me Under the Marquee*. And finally, in first position, our number 1 hit of the week—*Cymbal of Love*! That concludes our countdown for this week's top ten hits. You're listening to Radio WQRV, and I'm Rockin' Robin . . . .

34 THE ZOO & PETS

1 WHAT'S THAT? A mother and son are at the zoo. Listen and choose the animals they're looking at.

NARRATOR: Number 1.
SON: That's the longest neck I've ever seen!
MOTHER: Its legs are long too.

NARRATOR: Number 2.
SON: What's that on its back?
MOTHER: It's called a hump.

NARRATOR: Number 3.
SON: Is it dangerous?
MOTHER: Yes. It's very heavy and just look at those tusks!

NARRATOR: Number 4.
SON: What are those things on its head called?
MOTHER: They're called antlers.

NARRATOR: Number 5.
SON: Oh, how cute! What is it?
MOTHER: It's a very small bear that lives in Australia.

NARRATOR: Number 6.
SON: Is that a dog?
MOTHER: No. It looks a little like a dog. But it's not a pet.

NARRATOR: Number 7.
SON: Is that a tiger?
MOTHER: No. A tiger has stripes. This animal has spots.

NARRATOR: Number 8.
SON: Look at that big moneky!
MOTHER: Oh, that's much bigger and stronger than a monkey.

NARRATOR: Number 9.
SON: Oh, look! It has its baby with it.
MOTHER: Yes. It's in its pouch.

NARRATOR: Number 10.
SON: Are those antlers on its head?
MOTHER: No. They're horns.

35 THE FARM • FISH & SEA ANIMALS

1 WHAT'S THAT? A father and daughter are at the aquarium. Listen and choose the sea animals they're looking at.

NARRATOR: Number 1.
DAUGHTER: That looks like a snake!
FATHER: It really does look like a snake, but it isn't.

NARRATOR: Number 2.
DAUGHTER: Wow! That sure is big!
FATHER: I think it's the largest sea animal in the world.

NARRATOR: Number 3.
DAUGHTER: I've seen those black shells on the beach.
FATHER: That's right. And we've eaten the animal that lives inside too.

NARRATOR: Number 4.
DAUGHTER: Are those legs?
FATHER: No. They're called tentacles.

NARRATOR: Number 5.
DAUGHTER: Wow! Look at how it jumps out of the water! Is it a shark?
FATHER: No. A shark doesn't jump like that.

NARRATOR: Number 6.
DAUGHTER: That's pretty.
FATHER: See its five arms?

NARRATOR: Number 7.
DAUGHTER: What's that red animal called?
FATHER: You know what that is. We've eaten it for dinner.

NARRATOR: Number 8.
DAUGHTER: Look at that animal lying on the rocks. It has whiskers. Can it swim?
FATHER: Yes, it can.

36 BIRDS • INSECTS & RODENTS

1 A NATURE WATCH. A woman is looking through a pair of field glasses. Listen and choose the things she sees.

NARRATOR: Number 1.
WOMAN: I see a big bird with a long neck.
MAN: Is it on land or water?
WOMAN: It's standing in the water.

NARRATOR: Number 2.
WOMAN: What a pretty bird!
MAN: What color is it?
WOMAN: It's blue.

NARRATOR: Number 3.
WOMAN: What a big bird!
MAN: What does it look like?
WOMAN: It's very dark, and it has a big beak.

NARRATOR: Number 4.
WOMAN: There's a black bird.
MAN: Is it big or small?
WOMAN: It isn't big and it isn't small. It's medium.

NARRATOR: Number 5.
WOMAN: That's a pretty bird. It's small and has red feathers.
MAN: Where is it red?
WOMAN: Only in front.

NARRATOR: Number 6.
WOMAN: That bird is really beautiful. It's white and has a yellow crest.

NARRATOR: Number 7.
WOMAN: Oh, I see a small animal. It's eating some kind of insect.
MAN: Is it a rat?
WOMAN: It looks like a rat, but it's much smaller than a rat.

NARRATOR: Number 8.
MAN: Is that a squirrel?
WOMAN: I don't think so. It's striped, and I've never seen a striped squirrel.

37 SPACE • THE MILITARY

1 A SCIENCE LESSON. Professor Latham is talking about space. Listen and choose the things he's describing.

NARRATOR: Number 1.
PROFESSOR: There are million and millions of them in the universe. And each one consists of millions and millions of stars.

NARRATOR: Number 2.
PROFESSOR: It's the Earth's natural satellite, and it moves around the Earth every 28 days. Apart from the Sun, it's the brightest object in our sky.

NARRATOR: Number 3.
PROFESSOR: It's a very, very large star and has a temperature of about 6,000 degrees Centigrade. Its light reaches the Earth in 8.3 minutes. All nine planets in our solar system move around it in space.

NARRATOR: Number 4.
PROFESSOR: It's the planet on which we live. It's 93 million miles from the Sun and has a year of 365 days. We believe it's the only planet in our solar system on which people live.

NARRATOR: Number 5.
PROFESSOR: Because this planet is farther away from the Sun than the Earth is, it is very, very cold. It's easy to recognize this planet because of its beautiful rings.

38 HOBBIES & GAMES • SEWING & SUNDRIES

1 WHAT ARE THEY DOING? Listen and circle the correct answer.

NARRATOR: Number 1.
WOMAN: Do we have any tissue paper?
MAN: Yes. There's some in the drawer.

NARRATOR: Number 2.
MAN: I'm bored.
WOMAN: Why don't you get the cards?

NARRATOR: Number 3.
WOMAN: Is that a pelican or a stork?
MAN: I think it's a pelican.

NARRATOR: Number 4.
WOMAN: I have to draw a circle.
MAN: Here, why don't you use this?

NARRATOR: Number 5.
MAN: This piece of material is too big.
WOMAN: Why don't you cut it with this?

NARRATOR: Number 6.
WOMAN: This is a very old penny.
MAN: Can I see it?
WOMAN: Sure. Here's the magnifying glass.

NARRATOR: Number 7.
MAN: Is that a star or the planet Venus?
WOMAN: I think it's Venus.

NARRATOR: Number 8.
WOMAN: What are you making?
MAN: A chair.

ANSWER KEY

1 NUMBERS • TIME

1

	First Turn	Back Stretch	Far Turn	Final Stretch	Finish
Lucky Lady	2nd	3rd	4th	4th	4th
Prince Charming	1st	1st	1st	1st	2nd
Fast Buck	3rd	4th	3rd	2nd	1st
Mad Hatter	4th	2nd	2nd	3rd	3rd

2
2. three fifteen
3. eight thirty
4. two forty-five
5. seven fifteen
6. five fifty
7. four forty-five
8. six forty
9. one twenty-one
10. ten ten

3
2. one quarter
3. one third
4. three quarters

4 Welcome to this workbook. We hope you like it.

5
2. 55% + 45% = 100%
3. 3/4 − 1/4 = 1/2
4. 4 × 5 = 20
5. 50 ÷ 2 = 25
6. 75% + 25% = 100%
7. 1/4 + 1/2 = 3/4
8. 1/2 − 1/4 = 1/4
9. 50 − 15 = 35
10. 3 × 30 = 90

6 number of women = 500
Prefer a digital watch: total = 400, 275 men, 125 women
Prefer an analog watch: total = 600, 225 men, 375 women

2 CALENDAR • HOLIDAYS

1
1. 26(th)
2. Tuesday
3. Wednesday
4. Friday, 29(th)
5. Monday, 1(st) 8:00

2
2. Happy New Year.
3. Merry Christmas.
4. We celebrate Independence Day on July 4th.
5. School starts in September.
6. My favorite day is Saturday.
7. We have a date for Thursday, the 28th of November.
8. Graduation is on Sunday, June 10, 1990.
9. Happy Mother's Day.
10. Is Thanksgiving on Thursday, November 24th?

3–5 Answers will vary.

3 WEATHER & SEASONS

1
2. 0
3. clear
4. sunny
5. 40
6. 3
7. cloudy
8. cold
9. below
10. freezing
11. windy
12. stormy
13. foggy
14. icy
15. warmer
16. 40s
17. warmer
18. 50s
19. winter
20. spring

2
3. I (Answers will vary.)
4. I (Answers will vary.)
5. I (Answers will vary.)
6. P
7. I (Answers will vary.)
8. I (Answers will vary.)
9. P
10. P

3 Answers will vary.

4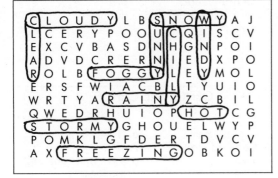

4 SHAPES & MEASUREMENTS

1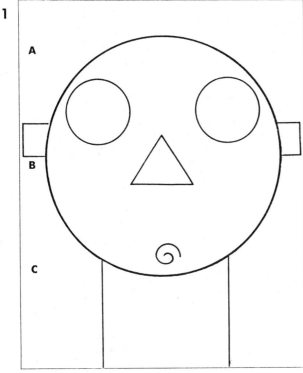

A

B

C

2 3. inches high, feet, inches long, feet, inch wide
4. inches high, width, feet, inches, depth, feet
5. feet, inches wide, feet, inches long
6. height, inches, width, inches, depth, inches

3 2. A

7.

3. A

8.

4.

9.

5.

10.

6.

5 MONEY & BANKING

1 2. True
3. False
4. True
5. True

6. True
7. False
8. False

2 2. e
3. d
4. c

5. f
6. b

3 2. D, E
3. D, D, E, E, E, F, F, H, H, H
4. E, E
5. A, A, D, D
6. A, A, A, A, C
7. A, D, D, D, E, E, E, F
8. E
9. D, D, D, E, F, F
10. B, D, D, E, E, E, F, F

4 Answers will vary.

6 THE WORLD • THE UNITED STATES • CANADA

1 Peru
Pacific Ocean
Bolivia

Argentina
Brazil
Atlantic Ocean

2 2. Europe and Asia
3. Europe
4. Africa
5. Asia
6. South America
7. North America
8. Asia

9. South America
10. Europe
11. North America
12. Asia
13. Africa
14. Asia

3 2. east, west, south
3. east, south, west
4. west, north
5. west, north, east, south
6. east, west
7. west, east, south
8. south, west

4 2. Nevada
3. Wyoming
4. Arizona
5. New Mexico
6. North Dakota
7. Nebraska
8. Texas
9. Missouri
10. Louisiana
11. Illinois
12. Michigan
13. Indiana
14. Tennessee

15. Mississippi
16. Florida
17. West Virginia
18. South Carolina
19. Maryland
20. New Jersey
21. New York
22. Connecticut
23. Massachusetts
24. Maine
25. Hawaii

7 THE CITY

1 Picture 2

2
- 2. bus stop
- 3. bus lane
- 4. stop sign
- 5. walk sign
- 6. phone booth
- 7. office building
- 8. traffic light
- 9. sidewalk
- 10. newsstand

3

```
S T F D E B U S L M R G O C
U A U M O O T H T A X K O N U
B H T R C T B V Y G J R E P O L R
W Y R C T S L K R E X I T J B
A D A V A A P Y E Q I A G L T
Y N S J L C Y O T R A F F I C
M A H C S K G L I M N B V L X Z
U N C S P E D E S T R I A N
T T E I Z R B W E S P O I G
F D N Q G K C R H O D F S A K
L C T W N B B U I L D I N G C
D V N B C E T A R M U T H D E
A I O E P H O N E B O O T H G
```

4

A	B	C
2. taxi	1. sidewalk	1. office building
3. subway	2. crosswalk	2. skyscraper
4. car	3. street	3. street light
	4. curb	4. traffic light

5 Answers will vary.

8 THE SUPERMARKET • FRUIT • VEGETABLES

1 pork chops, chicken, steak, milk, eggs, butter, cheese, frozen orange juice, frozen vegetables, tuna fish, soup, bread, crackers, lettuce, celery, potatoes, grapes, bananas, strawberries, mango

2–3 Answers will vary.

9 THE MENU • FAST FOODS & SNACKS

1 Lisa: salad, pork chops and carrots, jello, coffee
Peter: shrimp cocktail, soup, steak and a baked potato, cherry pie, tea

2 Answers will vary.

3
- 2. onion
- 3. donut
- 4. gum
- 5. soup
- 6. carrots
- 7. fish
- 8. fish

4
- 2. steak
- 3. pie
- 4. tea
- 5. pickles
- 6. fish
- 7. spaghetti
- 8. green beans
- 9. onions
- 10. hamburger
- 11. hot dog
- 12. salad

5
- 2. soft drink/soda
- 3. steak, hamburger
- 4. carrots
- 5. 679
- 6. donut

10 THE POST OFFICE THE OFFICE

1
- 2. Express mail.
- 3. Certified mail.
- 4. Two.
- 5. One.
- 6. Ten.
- 7. Six.
- 8. Five pens and eight pencils.

2
- 2. paper clip holder
- 3. typewriter
- 4. stapler
- 5. file cabinet
- 6. tape dispenser

3 Answers will vary.

4
- 2. True
- 3. False. It's next to the desk.
- 4. False. It's behind her.
- 5. False. The paper clip holder is next to the stationery.
- 6. False. The file folders are on the file cabinet.
- 7. True
- 8. False. It's on the receptionist's desk.

11 THE BODY • ACTION AT THE GYM

1
- 2. B
- 3. A
- 4. A
- 5. A
- 6. B
- 7. B
- 8. B

2
- 2. hand
- 3. foot
- 4. knee
- 5. lip
- 6. wrist
- 7. arm

3 Answers will vary.

4
- 2. False. He's walking.
- 3. False. He's running.
- 4. False. She's hopping.
- 5. False. She's swinging.
- 6. True
- 7. False. She's catching the ball.
- 8. False. He's throwing the ball.
- 9. False. He's pushing the table.
- 10. True

12 COSMETICS & TOILETRIES • ACTION AT HOME

1
- 1. blush
- 2. eye shadow
- 3. eyebrow pencil
- 4. eyeliner
- 5. mascara
- 6. lipstick

2 b. I cook breakfast. j. I eat breakfast.
c. I watch TV. k. I go to bed.
d. I take a shower. l. I put on makeup
e. I wake up. (lipstick).
f. I shave. m. I put on after-shave.
g. I get dressed. n. I shampoo my hair.
h. I brush my hair. o. I wash my face.
i. I brush my teeth. p. I take a bath.

3 Answers will vary.

4 2. lipstick 5. after-shave
3. cologne 6. comb
4. brush

13 ACTION AT SCHOOL

1 2. b 7. g
3. f 8. j
4. e 9. a
5. d 10. i
6. h

2 Answers will vary.

3 2. pointing 6. reading
3. erasing 7. picking up
4. giving 8. tearing up
5. taking

4 2. False. He's standing.
3. True
4. False. He's cutting a piece of paper.
5. False. He's drawing.

14 THE DOCTOR • THE DENTIST

1 2. The Dentist's 6. The Dentist's
3. The Dentist's 7. The Doctor's
4. The Doctor's 8. The Dentist's
5. The Dentist's

2 2. scale 4. thermometer
3. x-ray 5. toothpaste

3 2. dental assistant 5. drill
3. filling 6. overbite
4. Novocain 7. braces

4 2. The doctor gave me a prescription for my high
blood pressure.
3. She used dental floss for the food between her
teeth.
4. He used a Band-Aid for his cut.

15 OCCUPATIONS • THE FAMILY • EMOTIONS

1 1. father's
2. father, mother, angry, teacher
3. computer technician
4. father, proud
5. brother, artist
6. Maria, confused
7. nurse, teller
8. journalist, shy
9. cousin, teller, loves (likes)
10. annoyed, veterinarian

2 2. father 5. father-in-law
3. aunt 6. grandson
4. sister-in-law 7. daughter-in-law

3 2. d
3. a
4. b

Positive: ecstatic, pleased, happy
Negative: sad, displeased, miserable, ashamed

4 Answers will vary.

16 OPPOSITES

1 Picture 2

2 2. dirty 6. light
3. hot 7. straight
4. old 8. open
5. messy

3 2. True
3. False. Horses are faster than dogs.
4. True
5. True
6. False. A child is younger than its mother.
7. False. Fire is hotter than ice.
8. True
9. False. Cars are slower than planes.
10. False. Cats are older than kittens.
11. False. February is shorter than March.
12. True

4 2. shorter
3. tallest
4. shortest
5. younger
6. younger
7. youngest
8. oldest
10. Elm Street is wider than Oak Street.
11. Elm Street is narrower than Main Street.
12. Oak Street is the narrowest.
13. Main Street is the widest.

17 MEN'S WEAR • WOMEN'S WEAR

1 Pictures 2, 5, 7

2
2. True
3. False. He's wearing a checked sport shirt.
4. False. She's carrying a clutch bag.
5. False. She's carrying a handbag.
6. False. She's wearing slacks (pants).
7. True
8. False. They're purple.
9. False. They're blue.
10. False. She's wearing a yellow sweatshirt.

18 MEN'S & WOMEN'S WEAR • ACCESSORIES

1
2. $14.99	12. $29.99
4. $12.99	13. $6.99
8. $30.99	14. $25.99
10. $175.00	17. $7.99
11. $15.99	

2
2. watch	5. cap
3. scarf	6. gloves
4. ring	

3 ear, ring, turtle, neck, rain, coat, under, shirt, tie, pin

3. ear
4. tie
5. ring, neck
6. turtle
7. rain
8. pin, coat
9. shirt, under

19 HOUSING • THE BACKYARD AND GARDEN

1 *Type of House or Building:* ranch

Inside: dining room, 3–4 bedrooms, 3–4 bathrooms, large kitchen

Outside: garage, patio, lawn, backyard

House 3

2
2. False. It has a patio.
3. True
4. True
5. False. It has a (large) garden.
6. False. It's for rent.
7. False. It has a one-car garage.
8. True

3
2. lawn mower	6. umbrella
3. watering can	7. lounge chair
4. trowel	8. elevator
5. barbecue	9. closet

4
2. watering can	5. garage
3. hedge	6. hall
4. kitchen	

20 THE LIVING ROOM • THE DINING ROOM • THE BEDROOM • THE BATHROOM

1
2. Living Room	6. Bathroom
3. Bedroom	7. Living Room
4. Bathroom	8. Dining Room
5. Bedroom	

2
2. A mattress is softer than the floor.
3. A quilt is warmer than a sheet.
4. A bath towel is wider than a hand towel.

3
Sofa	$1,300	$799
Love seat	$1,250	$750
Club chair	$450	$279
Ottoman	$300	$199
Coffee table	$429	$299
End table	$350	$250
Wall unit	$900	$600
Lamp	$150	$ 75
Mirror	$120	$ 65
Carpet	$729	$399

4
2. False. It's next to the window.
3. True
4. True
5. False. They're above the plates.
6. False. They're striped.
7. False. There's a mirror over the sideboard.
8. True
9. False. The knife is longer than the soupspoon.

21 THE KITCHEN • KITCHENWARE

1 2, 5, 7, 8

2
2. A food processor is faster than a knife.
3. Aluminum foil is heavier than plastic wrap.
4. A toaster oven is slower than a microwave oven.

3
2. b	7. a
3. c	8. c
4. a	9. c
5. c	10. a
6. b	

4
2. ladle	5. knife
3. whisk	6. peeler
4. strainer	

2 *Possible answers:*

2. In kitchen A the freezer is on the side of the refrigerator, but in kitchen B the freezer is on top of the refrigerator.
3. Kitchen A has three cupboards. Kitchen B has four cupboards.
4. The stove in kitchen A has three burners. The stove in kitchen B has four burners.
5. Kitchen A has a spice rack over the stove. Kitchen B has a spice rack over the counter.
6. In kitchen A the cabinet handles are on the left of the cabinets, but in kitchen B the handles are in the middle of the cabinets.

22 THE NURSERY • THE PLAYGROUND

1
1. $55.00
2. $100.00
3. $30.00, green
4. $100.00, yellow
5. $75.00
6. $100.00
7. $100.00

2
2. chest
3. pail
4. kite
5. sand
6. clothes
skateboard
7. lamp
8. slide
9. swing
10. bear

23 THE LAUNDRY ROOM • TOOLS • CONSTRUCTION

1
2. c
3. b
4. b
5. b
6. b
7. c
8. b
9. c
10. b

2
2. False. It's on the shelf.
3. True
4. False. It's yellow.
5. False. It's on the bucket.
6. False. The vacuum cleaner has a plug.
7. True

3
2. wheelbarrow
3. hook
4. level
5. cement
6. trowel

24 ELECTRONICS

1
Video Cameras
Cassette Decks
Compact Discs
Clock Radios
Cassette Players
Telephones
Electronic Typewriters

2
2. False. It doesn't come with batteries. They're extra.
3. False. You can save (exactly) $60.00.
4. False. It comes in four different colors.
5. True
6. True

3

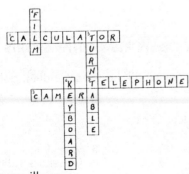

4 Answers will vary.

25 LAND & WATER

1
2. b
3. c
4. a
5. b
6. a

2
2. rock
3. dune
4. river
desert
5. lake
6. stream

3
2. lake
3. river
4. desert
5. waterfall
6. lake
7. mountains
8. lake

4
2. A desert is drier than a forest.
3. A lake is bigger than a pond.
4. A river is wider than a brook.
5. A waterfall is higher than a stream.
6. A river is deeper than a stream.

5 Message 2

26 THE CAR

1 gear shift, air filter, tires, turn signal, temperature gauge, windshield wipers

2
2. turn signal
3. speedometer
4. seat
5. gearshift
6. air filter

3 *Possible answers:*

2. Car A is a convertible. Car B is a sedan.
3. Car A is smaller than Car B.
4. Car A is newer than Car B.
5. Car B's tires are fine. Car A's front left tire is flat.
6. Car A's trunk is open. Car B's trunk is closed.
7. Car A has a license plate in front, but Car B doesn't.
8. Car B is missing a hubcap. Car A has all its hubcaps.

4
2. c
3. c
4. b
5. b
6. a

27 THE TRAIN, BUS & TAXI

1 *Bus:* $44, 4 hours, 4 stops, 5 departures
Train: $56, 3½ hours, 2 stops, 3 departures

2. more
3. bus
4. train (bus)
5. less (more)
6. bus (train)
7. bus (train)
8. more (less)
9. train (bus)
10. bus (train)
11. more (less)
12. train (bus)

Answers will vary for 13–16.

2
2. c
3. a
4. c
5. a
6. a

3 2. Utopia.
3. Libertyville.
4. The train from Libertyville.
5. The train to Springfield.
6. 9:00.

28 ROUTES & ROAD SIGNS

1 driving faster than speed limit
crossing double yellow line
driving through stop sign
turning left against no left turn sign

2 solid line   gray car
divider   45 speed limit sign
truck   curve sign
white car

3 2. c   6. a
3. c   7. c
4. c   8. a
5. b

29 THE AIRPORT

1 2. b   6. c
3. b   7. c
4. c   8. b
5. a

2 2. False. They work in the cockpit.
3. True
4. False. The customs officer looks in your luggage.
5. False. You select a seat before you board.
6. False. A helicopter has a tail, but it doesn't have wings. (It has a rotor.)
7. False. The pilot and co-pilot watch it.
8. True
9. False. They put it under the seat or in the overhead (luggage) compartment.
10. False. You have to show it to the customs officer.

3 2. skycap   5. cockpit
3. suitcase   6. carousel
4. hangar

4 waiting, jet, aisle, attendant, pilot

30 THE WATERFRONT • THE BEACH

1 2. c   6. a
3. b   7. c
4. b   8. a
5. c

2 2. (beach) blanket   6. lifeguard stand
3. (beach) towel   7. (beach) umbrella
4. (beach) chair   8. (beach) (sun) hat
5. lounge chair

3 2. boardwalk   5. Bathing suits
3. lifeguard   6. hat
4. seashells   7. beach

4 2. bow   7. freighter
3. barge   8. stern
4. ferry   9. pier
5. crane   10. line
6. deck
waterfront

5 2. A boardwalk is longer than a pier.
3. An ocean liner is bigger than a ferry.
4. A lounge chair is more comfortable than a lifeguard stand.
5. A rock is harder than sand.
6. A barge is flatter than a cargo ship.

31 WATER SPORTS • WINTER SPORTS

1 Water Sports, swimming, pool, ocean, snorkeling, boating, sailboat
Brochure 3

2 2. b   6. b
3. a   7. c
4. c   8. a
5. c

3 2. skater   6. snowmobile
3. diver   7. helmet
4. sail   8. rower
5. mast

4 2. water   5. surfboard
3. rowboat   6. surf (wave)
4. life jacket

5 2. White water rafting is more exciting than rowing.
3. Snowmobiling is faster than bobsledding.
4. Scuba diving is more difficult than snorkeling.
5. Figure skating is more interesting than ice skating.
6. Cross country skiing is colder than water skiing.
7. Downhill skiing is more dangerous than cross country skiing.
8. A ski cap is softer than a helmet.

32 SPECTATOR SPORTS • OTHER SPORTS

1 archery, volleyball, horseback riding, golf, hiking, tennis, bowling

2 referee, tent, stirrup

4 2. archery   5. volleyball
3. hiking   6. horseback riding
4. bowling

5 *Possible answers:*

2. They use rackets.
3. They use a net and a ball.
4. They make decisions in a game.
5. They protect the player.
6. They are used to hit a ball.
7. They are played on a field.
8. They run.
9. They use a net and a ball.
10. They use a ball.

---

33 ENTERTAINMENT • MUSICAL INSTRUMENTS

1 Cymbal of Love 1
Meet me under the Marquee 2
Heart Strings 3
Bad Brass 4
Tell It to the Trombone 5
On Stage with You 6
Winter Woodwinds 7
The Audience Has Gone Home 8
Dark Drums 9
I'm Just an Actress with You 10

2
2. xylophone
3. bassoon
4. accordian
5. harmonica
6. piano
7. cello
8. tuba

Strings: cello
Brass: tuba
Woodwinds: recorder, bassoon
Percussion: xylophone
Other: accordian, harmonica

3
2. a
3. c
4. c
5. c
6. a
7. a
8. b
9. b

4
2. ballet
3. ballerina
4. cello
5. instrument
6. ballet dancers
7. actors
8. theater
9. audience
10. stage

---

34 THE ZOO & PETS

1
2. a
3. c
4. b
5. a
6. b
7. b
8. a
9. b
10. c

2
2. False. A giraffe has the longest neck.
3. True
4. True

3
1. tiger
2. cat
3. paws
4. tail
5. whiskers
6. A cat is smaller than a tiger.
7. A tiger is stronger than a cat.
8. A tiger is more dangerous than a cat.

4
2. spot
3. pouch
4. fox
5. deer
rhinoceros
6. mane
7. bear
8. horn

---

35 THE FARM • FISH & SEA ANIMALS

1
2. c
3. c
4. b
5. c
6. a
7. c
8. b

2
2. b
3. f
4. a
5. c
6. e

3 bull, octopus, eel, kid, mane, clam, shark

2. kid
3. bull
4. shark
5. eel
6. turtle
7. angelfish
8. octopus

4
2. bulls ➝ cows
sheep's ➝ chickens'
farmhouse ➝ barn
wheat field ➝ vegetable field
a combine ➝ an irrigation system
baby kids ➝ baby lambs (sheep   lambs)
barn ➝ farmhouse

---

36 BIRDS • INSECTS & RODENTS

1
2. b
3. c
4. a
5. b
6. c
7. a
8. b

2
2. A duck is smaller than a swan, but a duckling is the smallest of all.
3. A ladybug is prettier than a spider, but a butterfly is the prettiest of all.

3
2. b
3. e
4. h
5. g
6. d
7. a
8. f

4
2. mosquito
3. butterfly
4. dragonfly
5. caterpillar
6. ladybug
7. spider
8. ant

37 SPACE • THE MILITARY

1
2. b
3. c
4. a
5. c

2
2. Earth
3. planets
4. galaxy
5. stars
6. Sun
7. Moon
8. astronauts
9. flag
10. Space

3
2. Venus
3. Pluto
4. Jupiter
5. Venus
6. Jupiter
7. Mercury
8. Jupiter. It's farther from the Sun.
9. Pluto
10. Saturn

4
2. b
3. c
4. a
5. d
6. c
7. c
8. b
9. a
10. c
11. d
12. b

38 HOBBIES & GAMES • SEWING & SUNDRIES

1
2. a
3. c
4. c
5. b
6. c
7. b
8. b

2
knit sweater 2
put tissue paper in box 3
put sweater in box 4
cover box with wrapping 5
put bow on box 6

3